THE LITTLE BOOK

Listening

Listening as a Radical Act of Love, Justice, Healing, and Transformation

SHARON BROWNING
DONNA DUFFEY
FRED MAGONDU
JOHN A. MOORE
PATRICIA A. WAY

Good Books
New York, New York

Good Books books may be purchased in bulk at special discounts for sales promotion, corporate gifts, fund-raising, or educational purposes. Special editions can also be created to specifications. For details, contact the Special Sales Department, Good Books, 307 West 36th Street, 11th Floor, New York, NY 10018 or info@skyhorsepublishing.com.

Good Books is an imprint of Skyhorse Publishing, Inc.®, a Delaware corporation.

Visit our website at www.goodbooks.com.

10 9 8 7 6 5 4 3 2 1

Library of Congress Cataloging-in-Publication Data is available on file.

Cover design: Kai Texel
Cover photo: Howard Zehr
Series editor: Barb Toews

Print ISBN: 978-1-68099-898-6
Ebook ISBN: 978-1-68099-913-6

Printed in the United States of America

Contents

Chapter 1
Listening: Generating the Possible

A new world is not only possible, she is on her way.
On a quiet day I can hear her breathing.

—Arundhati Roy

To listen—or to listen justly—is to intentionally launch ourselves into unknown territory, to dwell in the unfolding possibility of every encounter, with the desire and willingness to be changed. Welcome to this journey.

Listening is a small action with enormous impact. There is ample evidence in millennia of changes in the natural world, including among humans, that deep and lasting change often begins with small, nearly indiscernible shifts. To listen justly is to be a small catalyst of profound change.

Listening is not another tool in the communication toolbox; it is foundational to all personal and social change when it is done justly, equitably, and lovingly. Listening in this way is a deeper form of listening than our distracted, transactional ways of interacting with each other. It is an intentional, mindful practice of listening to both ourselves and others, aware of our internal processes, the impact of sociocultural factors on our communication styles, and the unconscious manifestations of ego that influence what is said, distort what is heard, and create a barrier to understanding. Listening justly entails being present in the moment, without judgment, agenda, or ego, and with curiosity and humility.

Many of us humans already believe that we are good listeners. We practice "active listening" by nodding, affirming, restating, or observing body language and believe that we are therefore doing it well. These are all good listening and communication skills but can be prescriptive and performative, preventing or delaying an authentic connection, trust, and understanding. We may be oblivious to interior mental states that are revealed in body language or fail to recognize that life experiences and cultural norms strongly impact how we display, guard, and sometimes even hide our emotional lives. We may be unaware that the listening habits we see as strengths are actually impediments to listening justly, such as offering unsolicited assessments, solutions, or advice.

To move beyond performative listening and other barriers to connection, we are challenged to become consciously aware of the assumptions, beliefs, and behaviors that feed our perceptions of separation and "otherness." Core values and mindful self-reflection must therefore ground our listening. At every step of communicating with ourselves or another, we can engage in mindful reflection rather than unconscious reaction or rote behaviors in order to listen with awareness and presence. From this

2

grounding, listening becomes radical in the original sense of the word: to affect the root or fundamental causes of our human difficulties in accepting and understanding each other. It transforms into an experience of justice, of entering into "right relationship," and also an act of love, providing a space of unconditional acceptance into which people can pour their stories.

Additionally, listening is a core component of healing individuals, communities, and the planet. One of the true gifts of listening in this way is that it is a profound and transformative experience for the one listening as well as the one who is being fully heard and held: everyone benefits by listening justly.

> "Being heard is so close to being loved that for the average person, they are almost indistinguishable."
> —David Augsberger

The benefit of listening in these ways is that they are adaptable to any setting in which there is a willingness to enter into meaningful communication. This includes listening to ourselves as well as listening in all of our daily interactions with family, friends, colleagues, people we don't know, and the natural world. It can be done in one-to-one interactions, as well as in group processes, such as professional collaborations, restorative and transformative justice practices, and other forms of conflict resolution. This book explores the many contexts, processes, and practices of listening justly.

The insights provided in this book are not about *only* listening. They also are guidance for speaking wholeheartedly and raising our voices as a moral necessity to name injustice, prevent harm, and invite healing dialogue. To do this with both integrity and efficacy, however, we must listen closely to our own pain and to the pain of those of us who are suffering, doing harm, and creating havoc and destruction for humanity and the planet through unconscious, unskillful behaviors. Listening with fierce compassion dissolves the barriers between us and allows undreamed solutions to emerge.

This book is organized to adapt to the reader's needs and interests. Listening is a nonlinear, circular process of constantly refining our listening skills as we ground ourselves in core values, cultivate awareness, listen, respond, learn, and then try again. The goal is increased awareness: we are always becoming better listeners. The process is the point. The chapters can therefore be read sequentially, or you may wish to skip back and forth among them. Listen to your own needs and longings and explore the book in whatever way resonates with you.

The next two chapters are foundational: Chapter 2 provides a glance at the growing evidence from many fields that listening has profound implications for our individual, collective, and planetary well-being. Chapter 3 turns to an exploration of the core values that are the bedrock of just listening. Chapter 4 makes the transition from listening foundations to listening as praxis: a collection of practices intended to make change in the world. The following chapters, 5 through 9, focus on one of these practices at a time: self-reflection, identifying challenges, responding wholeheartedly, self-care, and listening to transform harm. At the end of these chapters you will find recommendations for relevant "micro" practices to try. Stories throughout the book illustrate practices and featured listening concepts. We tie all of this together in Chapter 10, closing with a reflection on the quantum power of listening to birth social change and to transform our world into one of harmony and wholeness, ushering in the possible.

It is important to note that, when we use the words "listening," "just listening," or "listening justly" throughout the book, we mean these various ways and capacities of listening.

The information and methods outlined in this book are based on current evidence-based research and cutting-edge advances in a range of fields, from social and neurosciences and evolutionary biology, to emergent inter-spiritual insights. This work is unfolding rapidly, even since the inception of this writing project. Therefore, this content is offered generously, with humble awareness that it is incomplete. It is our hope that these perspectives and practices will continue to expand and be enriched by others' contributions. Take this book and make it your own, adapting it to reflect cultural norms, insights, and new understandings as they arise.

About the Authors and Contributors

This Little Book is a collaborative labor of love by a team of "Listeners," connected with each other through a program called JUST Listening. JUST Listening provides communication training to public benefit organizations and supports multiple volunteer programs that offer listening in spaces where people who are rarely listened to gather. The largest of these volunteer programs is at the

State Correctional Institution (SCI) at Phoenix, in the suburbs of Philadelphia, Pennsylvania, where a core team of incarcerated and non-incarcerated Listeners has developed a customized listening curriculum. In our work together, over two hundred incarcerated people at the prison were trained as Listeners from 2016 to 2020, when the COVID-19 pandemic closed the prison to outside volunteers. The intense prison environment simply magnifies the challenges all of us encounter in our daily interactions. Stories and insights gained from this collaboration are scattered throughout the book and are relevant for all of us, whether or not we have any personal experience of carceral settings.

All of the contributors and coauthors of this book have completed training on how to listen justly as elucidated in this book, including Listeners who are incarcerated at SCI-Phoenix. Although isolated from one another during the pandemic, we worked across the divide of quarantines, prison walls, and later, international borders, to write this book. The many stories, quotes, and practices that punctuate the following chapters come from the direct experience of all of us, true collaborators in this effort. Occasionally in the book, we use the term "JL Listener" to refer to one of us authors or contributors.

> "My improved listening has allowed others to be more open, more honest, and more expressive with me, resulting in better relationships. Every conversation is an opportunity for growth."
> —JL Listener

The Possible

We are living in extremely challenging times, collectively experiencing chaotic, toxic, and divisive interpersonal and systemic upheaval. We are reminded every day that many social interactions around the globe are characterized by intolerance, contempt, hatred, and extreme binary thinking. In the midst of these disturbances, however, are also growing pockets of human activity that are moving us closer to a social order characterized by empathy, inclusion, equity, justice, and love. Listening justly is a small but essential and integral part of this movement into wholeness and unity, of being the change for which we long. The methods and practices articulated in this Little Book transform everyday encounters into potent vehicles for personal and social change and transformation. Every single human encounter can shift the scales and bend the moral arc of the universe toward justice.[1]

Every. Single. One.

"No dark fate determines the future. We do. Each day and each moment, we are able to create and re-create our lives and the very quality of human life on our planet. This is the power we wield."[2]

Let us embrace this power together as we journey through this book. Let us listen.

Chapter 2
Listening into a New Way of Being: The Evidence

If what we aspire to is justice for all, then let it be for all of creation.

—Robin Wall Kimmerer

In the past half century, listening research has expanded from an early focus on listening in the contexts of education and business to a wide variety of disciplines including biology, neurosciences, healthcare, behavioral and social sciences, conflict resolution, restorative and transformative justice, and spirituality. This chapter offers a glance at the current knowledge in areas where listening has demonstrably high impact and has served as a catalyst for personal, organizational, and systemic transformation.

Listening for Individual and Collective Well-Being

The need for social connection and belonging is a basic human need rooted in our neurobiology; we are hardwired for interdependence. Disconnection and the absence of meaningful social interaction not only cause emotional pain, they can result in physical pain, illness, early death, and potentially destructive behaviors. This has vast implications for individual physical and mental health, as well as societal well-being. Attempts to achieve belonging by "fitting in"—changing our authentic self to feel accepted—are personally and socially harmful. The alarming rise in white supremacy and other extremist and terrorist groups, for example, is reliant upon the intentional exploitation of fears and feelings of isolation.[1]

Miscommunication and feeling misunderstood, unheard, and unseen also cause physical and emotional stress, contributing to an already-high level of chronic stress in some cultures. The toxic consequences are again severe for both individuals and society at large and include: increased illness, difficulty in learning, lowered self-esteem, and increased perceptions of threat among many.[2]

Listening is the taproot of healthy relationship formation, nurturing a sense of belonging and trust: one vital way to address our collective dis-ease is to listen our way back to one another and our planet. There is ample evidence that listening provides a sense of agency for children, adults, and communities. Being heard facilitates emotional regulation and stability. When we are listened to, we display enhanced problem-solving ability, surfacing more innovative and alternative solutions than those generated alone. Listening and bearing witness are also demonstrably effective for integrating grief, healing trauma, reducing harm, and breaking cycles of addiction.[3]

Being in relationships in which we are heard, seen, and valued as we are is therefore essential for healthy human development and societies. As neuroscientist Mark Brady writes, listening "is supremely instrumental and essential for lifelong learning, neural plasticity, and for cultivating the empathy circuitry necessary for forming close connections."[4] Happily, in the midst of our fractured world, we can routinely build webs of connection and create listening spaces in which individuals and groups can experience safety, compassion, non-judgment, and empathy. We can listen our way into new and just ways of being . . . together.

Listening to Transform Conflict

New insights and evidence within the field of neurophysiology about our physiological responses to conflict and harm-doing are shaping how we structure practices intended to transform those responses. When we are hurt, insulted, blamed, threatened, or have our deeply held viewpoints challenged, our physiological circuitry shuts down, communication deteriorates, and our bodies create an intense biochemical cocktail designed for fight, flight, or freeze. In this primal state, our brains register the same degree of danger as if we were "being chased by a bear," and we cannot truly hear anyone.[5] This invaluable research is indispensable in cultivating intentional interpersonal and communal skills and practices to honor dignity, lower hostility, bridge divides, allow for dialogue, and generate peace.

Though listening is not the sole solution, being heard and understood can shift our cognitive chemistry so that conflict transformation and harm repair become possible and dignity violations, which under-gird so much of our conflict, begin to heal. Listening is thus foundational to the work of transforming conflict and harm.[6]

Specific practices for transforming conflict and harmful behaviors have been in use for millennia. In more recent times, these ancient forms of individual and communal healing have seeded a variety of transformative practices that are discussed in Chapter 9 through the lens of listening justly.

Listening to Nature

> "Paying attention acknowledges that we have some-thing to learn from intelligences other than our own . . . it takes humility to learn from other species."
> —Robin Wall Kimmerer

We live in the waning era of the Anthropocene, a time of unprecedented change in the natural world initiated by humans. Our separation from nature has made much of humanity deaf to the guidance available to us from the nonhumans with whom we are deeply, inextricably connected and interdependent. Thus, we are headed into climate and species crises of our own making. Authors from multiple fields are discussing our unique time as one of a great turning to a new paradigm: we are listening anew to ancient and emergent voices rooted in wholism and symbio-sis. Hope abounds when we look and listen.

Many cultures throughout the world have long attuned to the rhythms of the earth, absorbing the wisdom of the planet and living peaceably and sustainably upon it. Increasingly, more humans are embracing ancient insights from Native American, First Nations, and other Indigenous groups, recognizing that our future as a species depends upon humbly taking our place as fellow creatures, not masters, of earth. Our collective appreciation of the need to listen deeply to the more-than-human world and be instructed by and integrate its wisdom is growing rapidly as the pace of environmental change accelerates.[7]

The ways and wisdom of the more-than-human world provide a template for healthy communication: cooperation, collaboration, reciprocity, complementarity, and generosity. This guidance is available to us anywhere we find ourselves, even in the starkest environments: we have merely to pay attention, look, and listen. An incarcerated JL Listener finds unerring guidance for his life and relationships in his keen listening to the world around him. He shares: "How, you may ask, can someone in prison take a walk about nature? Yes, there are limits, but I have seen some astonishing things from behind a prison wall." As he walks, he listens from a stance of deep mutuality, recognizing simple interactions with the occasional bird, butterfly, blade of grass, or autumn leaves, as guidance and gift. Listening in this way has cultivated generous, nonjudgmental awareness for him: "When I walk in the yard, if someone is in need of an open ear, I am there to listen, to listen as an act of love." The world is full of wonder and guidance if we listen to it deeply.

Some of our most intractable human problems— racial injustice, planetary pollution, gross income inequality, hunger, violent extremism, and war—can find solutions in the intelligences and processes of the nonhuman world. But first, we need to listen, learn the language, and then live collaboratively into a new way of being in health and harmony with all life.

Listening to Transform Our World

We are all agents of transformation through whatever form of action we choose to offer to the world: transformative action is conscious, intentional, and rooted in love and healing. Whether our actions take private or public form, our capacity and willingness to listen to ourselves and each other determines whether our words and deeds generate health or toxicity.

> "We but mirror the world. All the tendencies present in the outer world are to be found in the world of our body. If we could change ourselves, the tendencies in the world would also change."
> —Mahatma Gandhi

The degree to which we are creating a just and peaceful world is directly proportional to the degree to which we engage in transformative practices in our own inner and outer lives. We must begin with ourselves: personal transformation occurs when we intentionally turn inward, become self-aware, and experience an internal shift. This includes dealing with and avoiding depleting behaviors that compromise our work and our health, as well as honestly examining our own propensity for dualistic thinking, subtle power and dominance dynamics, and egocentric behaviors that center self over the common good. Abandoning old patterns of blame, judgment, fear, and reactivity, we can be sources of love, forgiveness, cooperation, and healing.

The same is true organizationally. As with so many human endeavors, activist and advocacy groups have long suffered from egocentric leadership, hubris, unwillingness to listen to opposing views, competitiveness, and hierarchical organizational structures that are deaf to voices seeking inclusivity, equity, and collaboration. Some of the dysfunction in social change organizations can be attributed to these unconscious, unskillful behaviors.

Here too, however, there are clear signs of transformation: increasing numbers of social change groups are shifting to collaborative, inclusive, and equitable structures and cultures and placing a curative focus on well-being for all, both personally and organizationally. We now have clear evidence that supporting the inner well-being of changemakers is not only essential for their health, but it also boosts organizational capacity for innovation and collaboration, ultimately leading to more imaginative, creative, and effective solutions to social and environmental challenges.[8]

> "If we listen carefully enough . . . our bodies, the land, and circumstance will tell us what to do. If someone were to ask me what I would do about the problems in the world today, I would say, 'Listen. If you listen carefully enough, you will in time know exactly what to do.'"
>
> —Derek Jenson[9]

15

Listening is a dynamic, organic activity that we must intentionally reimagine and adapt as new research and insights into how humans process and integrate social interactions emerge. Listening justly is one of these reimaginings and can be done in our everyday encounters as we attempt to transform conflict and harm doing, and to heal our beleaguered planet and our relationship to it.

STORY

My daily self-care often finds me on walks in our county cemetery. Its tree-lined paths and roaming wildlife provide a tranquil setting for restoration of the body, mind, and spirit. I have found these walks especially restorative at this time of political and social unrest.

During one of my recent strolls, I noticed a man in a truck cruising along the paths. The bumper stickers on his truck were political and provocative in nature. I was curious as to why someone who seemed to be appreciating the same peace and tranquility had such divisive messages on his truck.

I flagged him down and asked him if we could talk. I mentioned my curiosity as to why he disliked the individual depicted on his bumper sticker. He immediately became defensive and said, "Why bother talking? You won't listen. You have your opinions; I have mine." I told him, "I miss the days when we could have conversations about differences of opinions on politics, and I genuinely would love to hear what you have to say." His response was,

"Ok, here is what I think," and he proceeded to share his opinions. When he was done, I reflected back to him what I heard. He replied, "Now that is what I'm talking about—you actually listened to me. You didn't argue with me or make me feel stupid; you listened." I then proceeded to express my opinions and he reciprocated a listening ear. Upon finishing our conversation, I said, "Ya know, we may have different positions, but we really have the same interests." His response back: "It has been a long time since I've had a conversation in which someone actually listened to my opinion without dismissing me. Thank you for this. It makes me want to talk again and rethink how I need to stop writing off people who may think differently than I do."

I may never see this man again. But listening is connecting. It was clear that we connected through the art of listening. An art that I hope we both continue to practice.

—Mary Jo Harwood
Trauma Therapist, Traumatic Stress Institute
Mediators Beyond Borders International

Chapter 3
Listening Justly: Foundational Values

Listening starts in the womb: it is the first foundational skill.

—Marva Shand McIntosh

L istening justly is a shift into a new paradigm of effective, transformative communication, moving from transactional and performative listening to reflective and equitable listening. When developing a listening discipline, we "ground ourselves" by becoming familiar with the values that undergird the practices of listening justly. Values provide guidance and direction to both individuals and groups; they are the roots of any endeavor from which corresponding practices and actions grow. Although ten values are listed separately below, they are interconnected and buttress each other. This list is also not conclusive: we have identified other important influences and considerations throughout this book and encourage all readers to add their own.

1. Justice

The dominant Western view of justice is legalistic and reflects a monolithic understanding of power: it is rooted in laws, rules, enforcement, and punishment, largely seen as the responsibility of the state. In many other cultures and indigenous groups, as well as in mediation and restorative and transformative justice, justice is relational. It is a justice that mends, heals, restores, and transforms, and creates the conditions needed for individuals and communities to live in "right relationship" with each other and the natural world. This deeply interpersonal understanding of justice is premised upon mutuality, respect, equity, compassion, and a recognition of our common humanity and dignity: it is therefore operative in all of our interactions.

"Listening is an act of justice. Oftentimes a person just wants to be heard. The listener need not have an agenda, an inclination to solve a problem or to impart feedback. Just listen. Being present in a place of coercive supervision, of violence and trauma, how much benefit can come from someone in crisis simply having someone to talk with who does not have an agenda or position of authority over the speaker? How much good might the same paradigm help in society?"

—JL Listener

Listening practitioners do not see themselves as a "voice for the voiceless." Those of us who are vulnerable and marginalized have voices; we are usually simply ignored. Rather, listening justly is intended to ensure that those voices are heard and amplified, thus honoring and acting on the truth of our interdependence and need to hear and learn from *all*. The focus is on accessing the internal strength and guidance of the individual and encouraging self-generated responses to that core wisdom. If we want a just world that is *for* everyone, we need to listen *with* everyone.

2. Emergence

Emergence is "the way complex systems and patterns arise out of a multiplicity of relatively simple interactions."[1] It is a process of coming into being—a shifting, a changing, an arising of what will be. It is challenging, therefore, to think of it as foundational to listening, since a "foundation" denotes something more solid, steady, or perhaps identifiable. Yet within this paradox lies enormous capacity for imagination, creativity, possibility, and growth, for both individual and social transformation. Conversations are how a new world is emerging.

Every listening encounter is an opportunity to invite or allow this possibility and growth if we approach it with a sense of spaciousness, creating room for the words, meanings, and stories to come into being as they arise. We unmoor ourselves from a prepared response or agenda of any kind. This can feel like falling into an abyss: "What will I say if I don't already know what I will say?" Yet in this abyss, something unknown is birthed. Emergent listening is listening in silent presence to what is being said, allowing it to take shape, and allowing our own responses to take form in real time. It is to trust listening as a generative process as it is happening, calling forth our mutual wisdom and knowing in the encounter.

21

3. Humility

Humility is literally to be of the *humus* or ground. Despite the hierarchies that we have formed in our social worlds, we are all human (again, of the *humus*), interconnected and interdependent, and made of the same cosmic- and earth-stuff. Rather than being self-deprecating or dehumanizing, humility is a radical equalizer that honors our common origins and our power as parts of a larger whole.

Despite our many labels (like supervisor and employee), roles (like parent and child), and stereotypes that lead us to think that we already know another—perhaps even anticipating what someone will say out of habit or repetition—we truly do not know. Listening with humility creates a greater capacity to see and hear each other beyond what we think we already know. When we listen from this place of profound unknowing and deep awareness of our own limited and unique perceptions of the world, we create enormous opportunities to learn from each other. Such radical humility invites us to explore as-yet-unknown possibilities together.

4. Curiosity

Curiosity is humility's close companion. When we shift into deep awareness of our own limitations of what we know, we can listen with a profound sense of curiosity.

Curiosity lifts us from the necessary grounding of humility into the gravitational pull of learning. We enter into a conversation not with ready answers but with a seeking heart, an opening for greater understanding. Curiosity quiets the dysfunctional ego, which would otherwise hamper our listening, and says, "I don't know but I would love to learn." As with emergence, curiosity can be spacious, allowing for whatever arises, but it can also be a place of more intentionality, where we ask questions to learn what we do not know. It can be incredibly powerful and revelatory to ask someone whom we think we already know, including ourselves, a question from a place of sincere unknowing and a desire to learn. It can be as world-opening as asking someone we do not know.

5. Dignity

Dignity, rather than the widely taken-for-granted notion of respect, is foundational to listening, especially in the work of repairing harm.[2] We may not respect our own or another person's harmful decisions or behavior, but neither of these diminish anyone's dignity or innate worth. Simply by virtue of being human we have value; we belong. If that belonging is disrupted by causing or experiencing harm, it is a disruption of our *sense* of dignity that is lost, not dignity itself. Dignity cannot be destroyed, given, or taken away. It simply is. Yet when we feel estranged from it, it is that dignity that calls us forth to do the work of healing and repairing. As author and restorative justice practitioner Danielle Sered so poignantly argues, to expect true accountability from someone who has caused harm is to honor that person's dignity, to recognize that they are part of our interconnected humanity and both capable and worthy of "doing sorry."[3]

> "Listening offers something that people in prison find healing: a no-judgment zone where they can feel safe enough to be themselves. We have learned that when we feel valued and heard, we are more open to seeking life affirming rather than violent solutions. We feel empowered to be creative rather than reactive and have more faith that these solutions can work. We are more able to visualize the good not only in ourselves, but in others."
>
> —JL Listener

This dynamic of reconnecting with our own worth is possible in all of us, no matter what relational "prison" we find ourselves in. We must be able to listen from the place of dignity within ourselves to the place of dignity within another if we are to identify and meet needs and implement true accountability together. Correspondingly, when we listen justly, the listening act is not only done with dignity, but it affirms the dignity of the person being heard as well as the listener.

6. Empathy and 7. Compassion

Empathetic listening occurs when we recognize the deep humanity of another and enter into their felt experience without judgment or manipulation. It is a process of "perspective getting," focusing intently on the experience of another and being willing to understand. We need to ask, not assume.

Empathy is not sympathy or pity, nor is it "walking in another's shoes." It is hearing, imagining, internalizing, and embracing the reality of how the other person experiences walking in their own shoes.

> "I need to learn how to listen to the story you tell about what it's like in your shoes and believe you even when it doesn't match my experiences."
> —Brené Brown [4]

Compassion is the daily practice of empathy: it is a movement of the heart toward another suffering creature. It is to "suffer with." Compassion springs from recognizing and accepting our shared vulnerability with other beings; it allows us to treat ourselves and others with loving kindness and discern whatever heart-centered response arises in the face of suffering. This can take the form of listening, and empathetic listening creates connection and healing.

Developing empathy and practicing compassion are not only necessary for good communication but are essential for the healthy functioning of all life globally. We are hardwired for empathy, but that extensive circuitry is activated only if we perceive the "other" as one of us, as included in our "we." [5] Not only are listeners vectors for increasing empathy in the human family, but the survival of our own species now requires that our "we" include the planet and all life on it.

8. Healing

The word healing means "to make whole." When we wholeheartedly open ourselves to hear another person who needs to share, we create wholeness together: there is a melding of hearts that satisfies a desire to be present, a need to be heard, and our shared need to be made whole. We all experience loss and grief; wounds from interpersonal and social-systemic

25

betrayal or harm; or feelings of inadequacy, loneliness, or estrangement from one another. Experiencing such harms can lead to a loss of meaning or put us out of touch with ourselves and our innate sense of dignity and worth. Listening heals and returns us to ourselves and each other.

One way that healing takes place is through narrative or stories that help us to make meaning of an experience of harm and integrate it into who we are becoming. These stories need listeners. Listening is therefore a "bearing witness" to a person's story. The listener is fully present to the harmed person, providing an opportunity for them to explore and articulate their experience in an atmosphere of safety and connection. Listeners create safe spaces of nonjudgment, compassion, and empathy to make healing their focus, reawakening us to our interconnected wholeness.

9. Community

We cannot survive without each other. Our home is Earth, and our very breath is made possible by our vast and literal conspiracy of interconnection. We con-spire, or breathe together, on planet Earth. Community is our very nature.

We must value community in order to (re)cultivate it in the midst of our estrangements from ourselves, each other, and nonhuman nature. The age of heroes and gurus is passing as we recognize the power and necessity of listening to every voice, learning from each other, rooting ourselves in our common humanity, and then acting together for the good of all. Community-oriented listening keeps us consistently grounded and connected to who we are as individuals and as coequal members of the human family on a shared planet.

We live in a time of collective trauma and despair that fracture our sense of community. But ours is also a time of remembering and reclaiming the universal organizing principle of connection and interbeing, not only as a goal but as a core value undergirding the process. This commitment motivates our central tasks: "to convert social isolation within our communities into connectedness and caring for the whole; to shift our conversations from the problems of community to the possibility of community, and to bring people together into conversations they are not used to having."[6]

10. Love

Listening is a profound act of love. Love has no condition: listeners meet people exactly where they are and provide a space of unconditional acceptance into which people can pour their stories. We simply need to be present, honor dignity, and hold compassionate space and reverence for whatever process another person is in. The only restrictions are the norms of all healthy human interaction: holding firm and not allowing boundary violations and no enablement of dysfunctional behaviors.

Listening justly sometimes means being the face of love for those who see nothing good in themselves, compounded by society's view of them as worthless and bad. If people whom society judges as "worthy" struggle with powerful feelings of unworthiness, how much greater is the struggle of those who are already so judged and convicted, systemically and interpersonally? Listening love is contagious. Those

27

who are listened to are infected with that love, and it begins to bloom and grow in them. Both listeners and those listened to report experiences of feeling "held," "cared for," and "loved." Listening with love is a profound and transformative experience for the one listening as well as the one who is being heard: everyone benefits.

As noted above, these ten foundational values are invitational; we encourage readers to consider each one and what it might concretely look like in your own life, and to maintain a sense of openness to other grounding values that may resonate with you as you move into the many listening practices that follow.

STORY

We went to Liberia to work with a group of marginalized and severely traumatized women from multiple ethnic groups who wanted to come together to strategize about how to improve their lives, especially to increase their livelihoods. We trained the initial group to facilitate dialogue in communities of brutally traumatized people, and in that training process, women discovered for themselves the importance of being vulnerable, of surfacing their own struggles with shame and blame. They learned that healing and empowerment can happen in safe spaces created to hear each other's stories: you could see the human connection emerge and the level of trust in each other grow. One woman commented: "What you made it possible to do is listen to each other in ways we hadn't before." Listening in the service of healing trauma and informal peacebuilding has concrete effects. Personal change can often generate societal change, and shared narratives can lead to transformation.

—Prabha Sankanarayan
CEO, Mediators Beyond Borders International

Chapter 4
Listening Praxis

If listening is to be a radical act of love, justice, healing, and transformation, it must be exactly that: an act. Not a pretense, a mere doing of something, or a thing to be accomplished, as our harried and productivity-oriented culture so often demands, but an animation of the foundational values in every listening encounter. It sometimes looks like stillness and silence; at other times it might be deeply engaged conversation. Regardless, it is no small undertaking, especially when grounded in the values outlined in the previous chapter.

This type of listening is different from our habitual ways of listening and being. It takes practice. But what do we practice?

The next chapters offer an in-depth exploration of five key practices:

1. Engaging in self-reflection and cultivating awareness, presence, and silence (Chapter 5)
2. Identifying, paying attention to, and dissolving impediments to listening (Chapter 6)
3. Reflecting, not reacting, when responding in both formal and informal conversations (Chapter 7)

4. Attending to self-care for healthful listening (Chapter 8)
5. Embodying, enacting, and transforming justice in our communities (Chapter 9)

The chapters also offer a set of related "micro" practices that provide options and greater detail for how to "practice the practice" in question. They are not formulaic or prescriptive but recommendations for how to develop a just listening habit.

Although a physical book necessitates a linear unfolding of these practices, they actually inform each other in much more circular ways, as the diagram below illustrates. It is therefore possible (even encouraged) to engage the following chapters in whatever order is intuitive for you: see what arises and resonates.

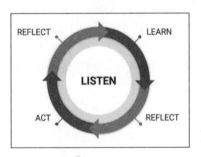

This diagram also reflects the shift from a listening practice to a just listening "praxis," which is "reflection and action upon the world in order to transform it."[1] We practice. We reflect. We respond. And then we reflect again and integrate what we are learning. Only then can we act upon the world for more intentional change—interpersonal and systemic—from a place of integrity with justice and love. This is what makes just listening practices radical in the original sense of the word: they relate to or affect the root causes of our human difficulties in accepting, hearing, and understanding each other. In fact, they transform listening from practice to praxis.

As you read the following five chapters, enjoy playing with and adapting the practices as your heart instructs and be sure to apply the foundational values to yourself as you try. Learning to listen justly is not about perfection. It is about being kind to ourselves as we learn something new, set new intentions, and create new ways of being. It is about opening up to all that is possible when we listen to ourselves, another, and nature with profound awareness and presence.

Chapter 5
The Heart of Listening: Self-Reflection

If we aren't practicing presence, we are practicing distraction.

—JL Listener

Just listening begins with self-knowledge, acquired by looking inward and becoming aware of our internal goings-on: our steady stream of thoughts, emotions, insights, physical sensations, and, with practice, the wisdom that resides in each of them. When we become conscious of ourselves, we can take stock of what is happening internally and use that information to make deliberate choices about how to respond in any situation, rather than react automatically.

The practice we employ to listen to our inner self is self-reflection. It is foundational to each of the listening practices in the following chapters: we need to be aware of what is happening in our own minds and bodies to identify any hindering listening habits, respond wholeheartedly, care for and listen to ourselves, and justly respond to harm-doing. Yet self-reflection is also a lifelong journey. It does not need to be (indeed cannot be) mastered before trying these other practices; they all mutually reinforce one another.

When we engage in self-reflection, we are facilitating three major elements of inner listening: *awareness*, which ripens into *presence*, and is nourished by *silence*. No matter who or where we are, the resulting insights can become the springboard for transformative listening in every encounter that in turn transforms our world.

Awareness

Awareness emerges when we are conscious of being conscious: it is a momentary stillness in which to examine our thoughts, feelings, and sensations as they arise and then reflect on what surfaces. It does not require a specific method; it is most simply about conscious noticing of this internal information and then pondering it. This process allows us to generate insight and understanding of our beliefs and behaviors, which then helps us to understand ourselves in our relations with others, making it a powerful tool for personal and systemic change. Awareness and reflection upon what arises are indispensable both for evaluating our own ways of doing and being, as well as developing sensitivities toward social and cultural differences. It is an awakening of mind and spirit.

Presence

While awareness is a waking up to the present moment, presence is intentionally bringing our whole self into conscious awareness of what is, and then staying in that state of spaciousness. The quality of our presence deepens and expands with increased awareness, intentionality, and reflection on what is happening. For example, when we begin to notice our internal selves, we will likely observe (in the present moment) that our minds are "off" in a past event, a future worry, things to do other than what we're doing, a judgment related to some other experience, or perhaps an unrelated bodily sensation. The more we become aware of these non-present thoughts within the present moment, the more we enter into the here and now. It is not a wrangling of the mind into submission; it is simply an awakened noticing, a more peaceful place from which to listen.

Conversations in which the listener is intentionally aware and more fully present can be transformative for the speaker as well as the listener. The speaker is provided the safety of a listening encounter free of agenda and judgment—born of awareness—and the gift of wholehearted attention—born of presence. Much is possible in such spaces: trust blooms, insight is born, and healing happens.

Silence

Silence can be fraught. It can be stressful for some, weaponized by others, or elusive for still others. Yet in the context of listening, silence is a gift. It becomes a habitual inner stillness that allows our state of presence to become fruitful. In this kind of silence, wisdom emerges—our own and that of whomever we are listening with.

> "I learned that I can help others more with my silence, rather than my interjections during conversations."
>
> —JL Listener

Silence allows us to enter into an awareness of ourselves in the moment *and* allows those with whom we are interacting to pause, reflect, and notice what arises from the depths of that silence: a lost memory, a deeper insight, a startling truth, a knowing—and discern their own creative response. It offers the possibility of emergent imaginings, insights, and connection.

Some cultures are better habituated to this practice than others; for some, being silent can be disturbing and challenging. But with practice, we can quiet our racing minds and deliberately slow the frenzied tempo of our daily lives. We learn to listen from the heart, not just with ourselves, but with others.

> "Call this level of listening generative listening, or listening from the emerging field of the future. This level of listening requires us to access our open heart and open will—our capacity to connect to the highest future possibility that wants to emerge."
>
> —Otto Scharmer

Self-reflection by itself does not automatically result in awareness, presence, and silence. We must set an intention to practice self-reflection daily so it develops into a habit. Although reactivity is automatic, we can use practices to pause, take a breath, and reflect briefly before responding in situations that activate and challenge us. In time, reflection becomes our default response. Set small goals; one practice and one small period of time, done repeatedly, will create the shift to listening more justly.

Burgeoning research from the fields of gender differences in communication, the neuroscience of conflict, and the science of empathy (exploring the role of mirror neurons, for example) provide essential, guiding insights that expand our ability to listen and communicate effectively from this place of self-reflection. There is evidence demonstrating that our bodies receive and generate physical signals and that our energy is literally contagious. Both positive and negative emotional states are easily transmitted to people around us.[1] It matters whether our minds are frenetic or calm, present or wandering all about.

The implications of this for listening from a place of awareness, presence, and silence are clear: we literally can be islands of peace—of stillness and spaciousness—in a turbulent world.

Self-Reflection Micro Practices

- Set a timer for three minutes and practice self-reflection: notice your in-the-moment thoughts, emotions, insights, or physical sensations, even if they are about non-present moments. Notice and reflect on them. What are they about? How did you feel? When the timer chimes, reflect on the degree to which you were able to listen and reflect. Gradually increase the time. Timers,

39

available as phone apps, can be set to sound randomly or regularly for this purpose.

- Pay attention to the sound of your own voice and the sensations in your mouth and throat when you speak. Do this as often as you can for a week. Becoming aware of our own physical speech will result in greater presence over time.
- Use opportunities in everyday life to practice becoming aware and moving into presence— e.g., waiting in a line, stopped in traffic, or waiting for an appointment or meeting to start. Become aware of your body and the energy coursing in and through you. Deepen and sustain your experience of it.
- Notice when you lose focus. Practice coming back to yourself and the moment when your mind wandered. Stay present and focused for fifteen to thirty seconds. Repeat often as this retrains the brain to be able to refocus more easily.
- Pay attention to what your body is telling you and how your body responds to your experiences. Do you feel tension in your stomach, head, or shoulders? Is there a resistance? Or do you feel pleasant sensations? Energized? The body is a guide.
- Breathe in order to be peace energetically. Pause. Take a few deep belly breaths and calm your body, mind, and spirit. Breathe in peace and let it fill your body. Notice your surroundings and intentionally breathe out peace and healing. Try this when you are with people who are agitated. Generously

envelop them with this calming energy. See what happens.

- Learn to identify your own feelings of vulnerability, discomfort, anxiety, anger, or resentment when in conversation with others. Notice when such feelings arise. When you do, stop, acknowledge the feeling, and reflect on what in *you*, not anyone else, generated the feeling.

- Practice silence. Next time you hear your inner voice say, "I don't know what to say," say nothing. Pause. Wait. See what bubbles up into your awareness, then respond from whatever arises in the silence.

STORY

My new cellie[2] was very troubled and extremely anxious. He'd had many cellies and had issues with all of them. It was not surprising that he wasn't too excited to get me, a stranger, as a cellie. But something strange has happened. He has since categorized me as a "great cellie," and we've become close friends! I believe that listening made the difference.

I noticed right out that he whined and complained about everything. This led me to know that he was hurting on the inside, needed to vent, and probably didn't have anyone to vent to or who was willing to listen. So I did what we do: I listened. I let him vent and was sympathetic to his plight. I learned that he had experienced a very traumatic life to the extent that his outlook on life became extremely negative.

He formed the belief that no one cared about him enough to give him the time of day. I would say that he felt that the world was deaf to him and his needs. He just needed someone to listen to him, to really hear him.

Listening had a miraculous effect in only a couple of days. For example, his high blood pressure, previously monitored daily, fell to normal after we became cellies, and now he's only being checked every other day. He told me that if it continues like that, he won't have to have it checked at all. He attributes the lowered blood pressure to the peace he has in the cell.

I am more convinced than ever that being heard is at the core of healing from trauma. In the aftermath of any trauma, the greatest need is to know that someone hears you or is open to listening to what you have been through.

—JL Listener

Chapter 6
Waking Up: Identifying Listening Hurdles

In trying to listen justly, I learned several things about myself: I'm judgmental, I have a desire to fix others who I perceive to be broken, and I'm quick to offer my unsolicited opinion.

—JL Listener

Though we wake up each morning, we often sleep-walk through our days, unaware of the world around us, each other, and importantly, of the many influences that impact how we interact and communicate with others. Much of our failure to understand what another person is communicating stems from our lack of awareness of several key factors that affect how we perceive and interpret what is said. It is distressingly easy to miscommunicate with another human: our spoken words pass through a treacherous labyrinth of challenges and filters before they land in the listener's consciousness.

By applying the elements of self-reflection (detailed in Chapter 5), we can pay attention to specific hurdles that impair our ability to listen. In this chapter, we explore common challenges to listening and cognitive filters that distort what we hear and offer guidance on how to identify them. These hurdles are multiple, predictable, and navigable. With practice, we can become conscious of them as they arise and make intentional choices about how to respond.

Challenges to Listening

Listening can seem like breathing, something we do naturally with ease and without conscious thought. Yet unconscious listening often means we are not listening at all, at least not effectively. Too often we are lost in the meanderings of our own minds or occupied by myriad distractions. To listen consciously and skillfully is more challenging than we might think; the first step to overcome listening challenges is to become aware of them, practice paying attention to them, and then minimize them.

Presuming We Know How to Listen

The first hurdle to clear is our own presumption that we already know how to listen. If we think about listening at all, we may feel that we give good advice, help people strategize problems, or express compassion by sharing a similar experience. We may have heard of active listening and practice it regularly.

Clinical psychologists Carl Rogers and Richard Faron coined the term "active listening" to describe a holistic, focused, and intentional form of therapeutic interaction. Since then, the method has undergone a popularization that has not only warped and diluted their original meaning but has become the default listening instruction. Unfortunately, this popularization has often turned "active listening" into a formulaic, performative, and transactional method of interaction that is inadequate for the tasks of healing, mending harm, and forging relationships.

> "I thought I was a terrific listener. . . . I offered my terrific advice, which seemed to be well received. But then I learned that my belief in my own listening ability was actually founded on several of the factors that create impediments to listening justly: my judgment, ego, and a need to 'fix' other people and to give unsolicited advice. Learning not to interrupt, to ask thoughtful questions, and to trust the power of silence were 'ear opening' for me."
>
> —JL Listener

The result is that we may underestimate the difficulties of listening and perceive ourselves as competent and effective listeners if we tick the boxes on a checklist of behaviors: open posture, nodding and other affirming gestures and sounds, restating and reflecting back to the speaker. Although genuinely motivated by a desire to understand, this performative approach to listening shifts our focus to ourselves and our performance as a listener and distracts from what is being said. To begin to listen justly, we must be open to rethinking how we have been listening up to this point and be willing to explore new and less prescriptive ways of engaging.

Perception, Bias, and Lack of Empathy

Perception, the ways in which we organize, interpret, and experience sensory information, is a complicated process that is affected by a host of physiological, psychological, and social factors. To further complicate matters, our perceptions arise from a constellation of cognitive biases, largely unconscious, that distort reality and muddle our communication. Because we interpret new experiences based on stored information from prior experiences, lack of self-awareness about our perceptions may lead us to make snap judgments about people or events, seeking only confirmation of our own biases and prejudices, devaluing or rejecting counterevidence, and interpreting experiences only in ways that are self-serving.

Such a lack of recognition and understanding of ourselves and others has a dramatic effect on how we (mis)communicate with others; it impairs true understanding and can have far-reaching, negative effects. Examples of our inability to listen through the distortion of our own perceptions and bias abound. This can be as simple as being distracted by our impatience or judgments when we hear a story with a different style than our own, be it more circular, repetitious, or linear than we are accustomed. Or it can be as dire as US medical doctors not hearing people of color when they describe their pain because of doctors' unconscious preconceived ideas about their tolerance for pain.[1]

Further, lack of awareness manifests as a lack of empathy for those we perceive as "other," and empathy is one of the most important elements of good communication. Despite the increase in global connectivity resulting from advances in digital communication, one study of students in the United States found that empathy decreased by 48 percent between 1979 and 2009.[2] Furthermore, in addition to the personal costs, there are vast political and societal implications for this erosion of empathy, and "no amount of law or regulation will overcome a lack of empathy."[3]

A critical element of listening is to practice making our unconscious thoughts conscious so that we can perceive accurately what is being communicated. When we listen, a stream of thoughts arises automatically in our minds, some of which are informed by these biases and judgments. They draw our attention away from what is being communicated, impairing effective communication. With awareness and practice, we can begin to notice these thoughts as they arise—notice and then return to present listening, notice again, and return to present listening, and so on. In this cycle, our unconscious biases move into our consciousness, the only place we can effectively change them. As our focus on present listening grows so does our capacity for empathy.

Multitasking

Despite a cultural insistence that multitasking is a necessary part of daily personal, social, and professional life, it is now well established that multitasking is impossible for most humans and it significantly impairs our performance and makes us more likely to make mistakes.[4] A hallmark of multitasking is task interruption. Our focused attention is persistently and frequently disrupted by the noises, visual intrusions, and addictive use of ubiquitous technologies. On average, it takes twenty-three minutes to refocus on a task once we have been interrupted,[5] and constant disruptions result in a state of continuous partial attention in which we never give our attention fully to anything or anyone. Research shows that these interruptions increase stress, disrupt healthy parent-child interactions, and result in higher rates of exhaustion, stress-induced ailments, and a doubling of error rates.[6]

Given the high level of misinterpretation and misunderstanding to which we are already prone, the acceptance and prevalence of multitasking and task interruption is another serious impediment to our ability to listen. We can't both listen justly and, for example, interface with any of our devices. We can't listen presently while also whittling down our to-do list. Happily, this habit is reversible through acquired skills of (re)focusing. To listen justly we must set our devices and duties aside and give our undivided attention.

Filters That Distort What We Hear

All of us have had the experience of witnessing or participating in communication blunders, exchanges in which what is said gets warped and twisted in its journey from the speaker's mouth to the listener's interpretive brain. The following are three distorting cognitive filters through which words and meaning pass and become mangled.

Inner Monologue

One of the barriers to listening is the content of our own minds, the approximately 6,200 thoughts that take shape in our minds each day.[7] The thoughts that come and go, some more rapidly than others, take our attention away from listening in the present moment. Often, when we think we are listening, we find that we have missed entire segments of a conversation because we have been drawn into our thinking, "wandering" mind.[8] We believe that we are listening, when in fact we are talking to ourselves. This inner monologue prevents us from giving our attention both to what someone is saying and to an awareness of our own inner guidance.

The content of this internal chatterbox is varied. We become distracted by our to-do lists and ruminate pointlessly about past, future, and (im)probable events. We find ourselves, mentally, in conversations with others: a conversation we just had, or plan to have later, or perhaps an entirely imaginary conversation. We can also get "lost" in memories when the person we are listening with mentions something that jogs a memory, and then we are off in the imagery of that place and time, rather than the present moment. Thoughts about our personal bodily needs also snag our attention, impairing our perceptions and judgment. That is, sleepiness, hunger, or any physical discomfort—or just our thoughts about them—can pull our attention away from listening.

Ego

Ego[9] is a provocative word often carrying a negative connotation. But a healthy ego is crucial to performing the daily work of being human: we can't function without it. Ego can, however, also be a dysfunctional filter that inhibits our capacity to listen, thus we do well to keep our egos in check.

The healthy ego, sometimes called our true self, is our core goodness and essence, characterized by love, compassion, peace, curiosity, and stability. The unhealthy ego, sometimes called our false self, however, wreaks havoc on our relationships. When caught unconsciously in ego's grip, we can become vain, boastful, negative, and trapped in our heads, replaying the same self-centered defensive loop over and over. Unhealthy ego responses are reactive rather than reflective, are largely unconscious, and can be both personal and collective, part of the norms and values associated with our group identities.

Some behaviors comprise a short list of our most common toxic egoic behaviors. For example, although interruption styles differ, interruption of a speaker is a pancultural phenomenon. This is not a benign habit: noncooperative interruption is deeply rooted in issues of dominance and power and has ramifications for gender, racial/ethnic, and class interactions. One aspect of this toxic dynamic is conversational narcissism, defined as "a person's tendency to insert themselves into the conversation, often with the desire to take over, do most of the talking, and turn the focus of the exchange to themselves."[10] We also silently judge our conversation partners based on real or perceived differences of any kind.

Common Egoic Behaviors
- Giving unsolicited advice
- Trying to fix someone's problem or situation
- Preparing an answer before the person has stopped talking
- Interrupting to say that a similar thing happened to you or someone you know
- Judging and finding fault with others
- Having a goal or agenda when in conversation
- Calling people names
- Exhibiting cultural arrogance

- Holding grudges
- Using us/them language or "othering" individuals or groups
- Displaying anger in a wounding way
- Interrupting others to make your point
- Needing to be right
- Taking things personally
- Confusing opinions with facts

Sociocultural Dynamics

Sociocultural differences that are signaled through a variety of cues can have a profound impact on how we communicate. Cues include such things as spoken language; body language; body size, comportment, and mobility; skin pigmentation; political positions; religious worldviews; and notions of time and space.

In some cultures, communication and information exchange is indirect and subtle, while in others it's more about exchanging ideas directly. Any listening method that does not acknowledge and embrace the rich diversity of human experience and expression is simply not useful and even potentially harmful in our interconnected, globalized world. The following sociocultural dynamics deserve our acute attention.

Social Identities

Every human on the planet lives at the intersection of multiple social identities: gender, age, religious affiliation, sexual orientation, body ability, race, ethnicity, class, education, and more. Each identity carries a host of perceptions, beliefs, and norms within it, making each person uniquely and beautifully complex. A white woman with little formal education

51

has different experience-generated perspectives than someone who is a college-educated, transgender person of color, for example. We all tend to identify with and favor those who have similar experiences and may alienate and discriminate against those we perceive as different from us.

An example of this is the "angry black woman" stereotype in American culture. Deborah Gray White notes that the stereotype is deeply rooted in American culture dating back to chattel slavery. Black women are characterized as "loud, irascible, too straightforward and just plain angry." A black woman's expression of anger is more likely to be attributed to her "angry" personality than to a justified, inciting situation. She will have a hard time being heard.[11]

Power and Privilege
Social identities also come with positional power and social privilege that inform what we hear and how we interpret it. Those of us who hold dominant social identities, like white, male, heterosexual, highly educated, and/or wealthy, have more positional power and social privilege. Without practiced self-reflection, such positionality impairs mutuality in communication, leading to assumptions that our perspectives and experiences are universal, superior, and more valid than those of people from marginalized groups. On the other hand, those of us from marginalized groups may be more likely to be or feel unheard or dismissed, and to experience other forms of discrimination in communication.

Even a sincere attempt at communication may fail where there is a power imbalance. It can nullify the speaker's response to the standard, "So what I hear you saying is . . ." comments of those sincerely believing they are engaged in "active listening." Such practices reflect a westernized approach to interaction, where control is located with the listener, for the listener's purposes, and on the listener's terms.

Body Language and Nonverbals
Both verbal and nonverbal expressions are complex, culturally coded, and influenced by so many known and unknown factors that our attempts at comprehension and interpretation are consistently unsatisfactory. There are no cultural universals relative to nonverbal expression. Although the four facial expressions of fear, sadness, happiness, and anger are coded similarly for all of humanity, how and when to display emotion is dictated by culture. The use of nods, gestures, eye contact, physical distance, posture, and other nonverbals are similarly fraught. Even "active listening," if rote and lacking awareness, ignores these sociocultural dynamics.

Different cultures have different normative ways of expressing emotion that do no harm; raised voices, highly animated exchanges, or on the contrary, polite and circuitous interactions are all coded differently throughout the planet. Without knowing what the coding is, listeners can misinterpret the interaction. In addition, implicit bias, unquestioned assumptions and perceptions, and lack of self-awareness about social and cultural blind spots lead to distorted interpretations of what is said.[12]

> "When we truly listen to each other, especially people different from ourselves, we see our similarities in the way we witness life—like our love for our children and the ways we love in general."
>
> —JL Listener

Interpersonal Dynamics

There are many interpersonal dynamics that impact how and what we hear. For example, although much is known about the different communication styles and needs of extroverts and introverts,[13] most interactions are structured to favor extroverts. A folk expression says: "If you don't know what an extrovert is thinking, you're not listening. If you don't know what an introvert is thinking, you haven't asked." Despite documentation that introverts require time to reflect and process before responding, we rarely provide opportunities for this in either individual conversations or group settings: extroverts dominate our interactions at home, in schools, at work, and in public life.

The magnitude and impact of these subtle complexities of human communication can seem daunting. However, once we become aware of the many hurdles that exist, we can reflect upon the ways they take shape in our own lives. We can identify our own listening habits, our social privileges and/or disadvantages, and the perceptions we have of ourselves and others, understanding that they all influence our interpretations of what we hear. With awareness and self-reflection, we can shift from unconscious to conscious listening and intentionally develop skills that make us less susceptible to these hurdles. Awareness, not perfection, is the goal. Only from this stance of radical humility can we listen justly with open hearts and ears. The next chapter goes into detail about the practice of responding wholeheartedly from this place of greater awareness and intentionality.

Micro Practices for Identifying and Self-Reflection on Listening Hurdles

- Before, every interaction, **W.A.I.T.**:

    Wake Up! Remember who and where you are. Become present.

    Be **A**ware of your own listening hindrances: clear and open your mind and heart.

    Be **I**ntentional. Intend to understand, focus, and be curious, nonjudgmental, and open. Open yourself to your inner guidance.

    Be **T**houghtful and **T**eachable. Respond consciously and intentionally. Reflect, don't react.

- Pay attention to your inner monologue during a conversation. Notice what thoughts are distracting you from being present in that moment. Release them and refocus on the conversation.

- Notice when common egoic behaviors surface in you while you are in conversation with others. Do not indulge your unhealthy egoic impulses. If you notice these behaviors in others, have compassion and do not allow yourself to get hooked into your own egoic reactivity.

- In a pair, have one person be the listener and the other the speaker. Set a timer for two minutes: speak and listen, notice, and then discuss what non-present thoughts arose for the listener while trying to listen. You might want to use a prompt for the speaker, such as "something that concerns me is . . ."

- Each day, select one listening challenge or filter to focus on and notice when it shows up in your conversations. Reflect on if and how you consciously responded and its impact on the interaction.
- Notice when you give, or want to give, unsolicited advice. Don't do it. Get curious and ask questions instead.
- Believe what the person says about their experience. When someone tells you how they feel, connect to that feeling, not to your own experience of and story about that emotion.
- In conversation with others, do not assume that you know what their experience is based on your own life story. Ask what the experience means to *them*.
- Practice strengthening your own empathy circuitry. One simple practice is open posture: sit at eye level with your conversation partner, not standing over or at a distance. Keep your arms relaxed, not folded across your chest. Invite eye contact (if it is nonthreatening both in your culture and that of your conversation partner).
- Watch your language. For example,
  - Learn and use the correct pronunciation of someone's name.
  - Honor everyone's choice of personal pronouns (she/her, he/him, they/them)
  - Use nonviolent speech: explore the use of violent similes and metaphors, figures of

speech, and expressions in the languages you speak. In English, for example, say something "hooked you," not "triggered" you or that you will "try" something, not "give it a shot."[14]

- Notice when you use "us or we/them" language. Make a list of who you include in your "we." Who is outside your circle, and why? Aim to expand your circle.
- Use inclusive rather than othering speech. For example, say "those of us who are unhoused," not "the homeless."

STORY

I was sitting in the waiting room of a crowded hospital in Eldoret, Kenya. I had just come back from Tanzania where I developed some sort of bacterial eye infection. As I waited to see a doctor, my mind turned to the Taturu people I had been visiting and working with and the experience I had in a totally new environment among people with a completely different culture from my own. I had been invited to a gathering in the village and sat among them. I at once noticed they spoke loudly and interrupted each other at will. To me it seemed chaotic and undisciplined. I found myself jumping to the judgment that one person should speak while the other listens without interrupting. I had the urge to "fix" them.

It dawned on me, mostly from my listening training, that this difference in culture created a barrier of understanding for me, which required listening justly. I had to be mindful of my sociocultural biases. I realized that I needed to maintain silence, to observe with humility and curiosity, and to learn and understand a different cultural style of communicating, not fix it. Silence was the precious sanctuary from which I could slow down time and observe and listen to myself and others in our interactions. When I felt the urge to offer my advice or felt judgment rising up in me, I would quell it with an alternative, more *just* thought. Allowing silence transformed an initially challenging dynamic into a new and deep learning experience. It has allowed our relationships to develop and flourish.

—JL Listener

Chapter 7
Reflection Not Reaction: Responding Wholeheartedly

Before you speak, let your words pass through three gates
At the first gate, ask yourself, "Is it true?"
At the second gate ask, "Is it necessary?"
At the third gate ask, "Is it kind?"

—Rumi

Listening justly is not only about listening. It is also about identifying the kind of conversation we are in and responding appropriately. Such responses grow out of self-reflection and waking up to our behaviors that impede good listening. We note what emerges within and between us as we listen and then we reply: sometimes with silence, sometimes with gratitude or affirmation, sometimes by asking evocative questions, and sometimes by sharing our own ways of seeing the world.

What follows is not meant to be formulaic or prescriptive ways of responding; rather, these various responses are offered to help us develop trust in the wisdom that emerges in the space that we give it. Some of the suggestions are useful for any conversation. Others have more relevance in conversations that are intentionally dialogic or have an explicit purpose, such as decision making or conflict transformation.

Identifying the Type of Encounter

Not all conversations or listening encounters are the same. Sometimes a listening encounter is a dialogue, an open-ended conversation of exploration and inquiry which is open to new ideas and ways of thinking and involves mutual sharing and understanding. At other times listening is less conversational: we might de-center ourselves, "sink in," and listen with another person, holding space more exclusively for what they need to say.

Regardless of the type of listening encounter we are in, we must be present and prepared to listen justly and know what is being asked of us in that encounter. We might ask ourselves:

- Is this a casual, light conversation?
- Is it one where I am expected to share as much as listen?
- Is it one where someone needs to tell their heart's story, be it a joy or a burden?
- Is it a decision-making process?
- Am I in the midst of a disagreement or conflict?
- What is being asked of me here?

Thus, one threshold skill for responding is recognizing what context or conversation we are in so that we can consciously and appropriately engage it.

Responding

If we are accustomed to engaging in conversation marked by the previously discussed listening hurdles, it can feel difficult to know what to do instead. We are tempted to fill silences quickly with default habits or rote responses. Just listening, however, is not quick or mechanical; we don't need to already and immediately know the answer or have a plan for responding. What is required is our willingness to be present in the moment and wait to see what emerges. This can feel intimidating and perhaps insufficient. It can help to know that the just listening praxis is already a wholehearted response for the ways it already honors the dignity of our conversation partner. We don't necessarily need to do anything more. The best form of responding is being fully, consciously, and intentionally focused on the encounter and waiting for a response to surface. In this section, we introduce several ways of responding that may arise and are consistent with the values and practices of just listening.

> "I've learned I already have the answers in me. This has helped me to see things from another perspective. I'm calmer, more patient, and less reactive. I think before I respond or make a decision."
> —JL Listener

Allowing Silence

Responses ideally begin with a silent, mindful pause. If we have cleared our minds to listen, then we are not at the same time preparing an answer (or off somewhere else in our thoughts). In silence, we let what we have heard enter us. Our consciousness catches up; we hear what was actually said instead of what we would have otherwise been simultaneously thinking. This creates an empty space into which a response arises.

It is tempting to fill the silence. Silence may feel awkward or anxiety-producing (until it becomes our default response). It may also feel challenging to trust that a response will arise. But it will, especially with practice. If the thought, "I don't know what to say" arises, then it is likely that more silence is needed. Sometimes, the best response is to say nothing.

"In prison, we only get 15 minutes for a phone call. It is challenging to listen justly in such a short time and with so much noise. I have developed the practice of being able to block out and ignore the noise when we need to. I sometimes allow time for intentional silence on the telephone. When I listen to my mother, I just let her talk, and I stopped interrupting her. I recognized this was her experience, not mine, and sometimes we don't talk at all. We don't need to say anything. We're just being. We're together."

—JL Listener

Expressing Gratitude and Affirmation

If you are not accustomed to silence or if an elongated silence does not feel appropriate, you can, in some instances, pause briefly to attune with a sense of gratitude. A simple "thank you" may be all that is needed. We might also practice: "Thank you for sharing your experience with me" or "I appreciate your willingness to speak your truth." Care is needed, however, because when someone puts words to a painful experience, they are not "sharing" that experience or the burden of that pain; we can thank them for their words but not for sharing something that is actually un-shareable.

We might instead sense that something more affirming, such as compassionately recognizing sorrow or joy, would be fitting: "It is brave for you to speak about what happened to you" or a heartfelt "I hear you." It can also be powerful, even courageous, to intentionally name what we are witnessing as affirmation, simply stating, "That is unjust." If someone expresses a feeling, as in, "That made me so angry" or "hurt my heart," we can affirm that feeling, saying, "Please tell me more about how angry you are" or "how that hurt your heart." Take care, however, to ensure that you are not imposing your own unconscious interpretation, assumptions, or judgments on someone's affect or conversational style, which can shut the conversation down. One way to address this risk is to ask a question instead: "Was that difficult?" or "Was that exciting?"

Be mindful of responses that are intended to be about gratitude and affirmation but are in fact evaluative opinions, such as "that was brilliant, thank you!" or "thank you for that intelligent comment." In group settings especially, we process such statements within our own framework, which can result in feelings of comparative worth or worthlessness, among other interpretations. Instead, we can affirm without judgment by expressing sincere gratitude for the fact that someone has shared a part of their life with us; witnessing, naming, and affirming what was spoken; and inviting more of what they want to say.

Asking Questions

Another response is simply to ask open-ended questions, which are questions that require more than a yes or no answer. Asking such a question can lead to deeper understanding and, when appropriate, helps to keep our conversation partner as the center of attention. Asking a question can also be a helpful replacement for the things we are more accustomed to doing in conversation, such as giving advice, trying to solve a problem, or "empathizing" by shifting the attention to a time we experienced something similar. If these habitual responses arise, we can notice them and then consciously redirect our response, asking a question seeking more information. Questions, even simple ones, if asked from a place of humility and curiosity, are transformative. We can learn something we did not know, even if we are engaging with someone we know well.

Asking questions can also help with decision making. We all have our own inner wisdom and to be asked, for example, what we want to do (or not) and why—and then be deeply heard in our response—is an incredibly generative process. Questions help us to create the world we want.

Questions can also help us heal harm and resolve conflict. Facilitators of restorative justice dialogues, for example, engage participants using open questions that draw out information about what happened, impacts of the harm-doing (e.g., physical, mental, emotional, or financial), ideas for how harm can be repaired, and future intentions. Listening to their responses helps the facilitator or circle keeper frame additional questions to guide them across the bridge from where they are to where they want to be.

New questions arise and are framed as the facilitators follow participants' lead.

Responses of every kind also must be premised upon trust; our own trustworthiness and actions that cultivate genuine trust within the conversation are more likely to build relationships and lead to understanding. Without trust, we are less likely to speak our own truth and allow ourselves to be vulnerable. Lack of trust precludes full, honest sharing, limits the healing and transformative potential of the conversation, and can even create or perpetuate misunderstanding.

Fran Peavey's Strategic Questioning method is designed to ask purposeful, non-egoic, nonjudgmental open questions that invite and elicit reflection, creative thinking and problem solving, and to achieve deep levels of understanding and insight for both speaker and listener. Open questions like these are intended to help the speaker explore their own reality, options, desires, and personal power. The following list of sample questions is derived from Peavey's work.[1]

Sample Open Questions

- What concerns you?
- What have you observed about this situation?
- How does it make you feel?
- Ideally, how would you like to see this issue resolved?
- What outcome would you like to see?
- What is your goal?
- How do you think this outcome/goal/resolution could happen? What ideas do you have?

(Continued on next page)

- Can you say more about that?
- What suggestion/additional suggestions do you have?
- What other possibilities can you imagine?
- What do you need?
- What assistance would you like?
- What next steps can you suggest?

Some of our habitual responses, such as those outlined below, are unskillful and even potentially toxic, inducing stress-responses in our conversation partners. With awareness and practice, these common difficulties can be avoided. Note also that it can be the *tone* of a question that makes it inappropriate.

Common Listening Responses and Alternatives

	Common Response	Try This Instead
Questions that are thinly veiled opinions or advice	Wouldn't it be better if you did [x]? Have you considered [x]?	Be quiet. Ask appropriate open questions, such as the samples listed above.
Questions/ comments that are argumentative, accusatory, or dismissive	I have a better idea. Whatever. The *real* issue is [x] What do you mean?	Ask questions grounded in genuine curiosity: What ideas do you have? What issues do you see? Can you say more about what you mean when you say . . .

	Common Response	Try This Instead
Comments that lack empathy	Don't feel that way . . .	I am here. Tell me how you feel.
	I'm sure it's not that bad . . . Yes, but . . .	Please tell me more about what you are going through.
	Well at least it wasn't worse.[2]	Would you like me to just sit with you?
		Where appropriate, offer engaged silence.
Comments attempting to fix, save, or change another person.[3]	You should . . . No, you're wrong. It's actually xyz. I know what to do. I'll handle it for you.	See the list of sample open questions above.
Comments that interpret or make assumptions about what was said	It sounds to me as if you are [name emotion]. So what I hear you saying is . . . I can tell that you are feeling angry.	How does that make you feel? What are you feeling? What does this mean to you? Ask open questions.

(Continued on next page)

	Common Response	Try This Instead
Comments that shift the focus to ourselves.	The same thing happened to me! I know exactly what you mean. Let me tell you about my experience . . .	Listening attentively and without ego. Remember it's not about you.

Understanding and Sharing

Sometimes we are in an encounter where we are expected to respond by sharing our own stories or perspectives in a dialogue. Unfortunately, what often passes for dialogue is simply an argument in which we try to convince others or demonstrate the rationality and rightness of our cause or perspective. We want to win. Such exchanges do not narrow the divides between us, they exacerbate them.

Dialogue is the antidote to this tendency: it is not about "winning" or "being right" but about transforming what we each know individually. In a dialogue, there is openness and reciprocity, a willingness to change our point of view and a desire to understand that of another. We don't need to agree. We need only be present, curious, abandon all judgment and expectation, and be open to what is possible. We meet on the common ground of our shared humanity.

Bernard Lee, SM,[4] offers guidelines for engaging in challenging conversations so that the dialogue heals, not wounds:

1. When we speak, our entire intention and reason for speaking is to help the other

person understand us. We speak to be understood, not to convince.

2. We listen with the purpose of understanding, not arguing or challenging. We let words have the meaning the other person gives to them, not ours: we are curious and ask what that is. We do not refute or argue with our partner, even internally.

3. We stay at the table, even if it gets uncomfortable. This builds trust and gives everyone permission to say what they need to say.

4. If we know information that supports the other side, we share it.

Sharing appropriate information is fine and can contribute to a greater understanding of issues and awareness of options. Giving unsolicited advice, however, is rarely welcome and can create resistance, resentment, dependency, and a lack of accountability. We own, act upon, and take responsibility for decisions and insights that are the fruit of our own discernment in ways that are not possible if our unique experiences, energies, and wisdom are not engaged in the process. To serve as a mirror for another person's process by responding with curiosity and compassionate inquiry is both gift and privilege.

With practice, we can adapt and listen justly, even in challenging situations. In crafting our responses, we once again take up the threads of listening's foundational values and self-reflection that are the warp and woof of healthy conversations.

Micro Practices for Responding Wholeheartedly

- Listen to yourself or another person with more silence than usual and with a deep sense of curiosity. Try to feel that curiosity physically in your body, breathing into a "clean slate" of unknowing.
- Following the pause that comes with silence, practice responding by simply expressing gratitude or affirmation, or ask the person you are listening with a question from a place of genuine curiosity. Use the sample open questions on pages 65-66 for guidance if you are stuck.
- With a partner, practice asking questions. Provide your partner with a prompt (e.g., something that concerns them or a story from childhood) and set a timer, giving them two minutes to talk about their response to the prompt. During that time or thereafter ask them a question or two or three. See where the conversation goes! This is a useful exercise in group and classroom settings.
- Think about a decision that you are trying to make. Write down some questions that would be helpful for you in considering options. With a partner, share the situation and ask them to ask you only the questions that you prepared; no advice, sharing similar situations, etc. Together, listen to your responses and listen to yourself as you speak your own wisdom in response to them. Afterwards, reflect on how generative the process was.

- Rather than directly challenge the beliefs and opinions of someone with whom you disagree, invite further conversation. Try something like: "I am curious about what in your experience has led you to that belief. Please tell me more about why you think that."

STORY

In 2018, 2,648 incarcerated men were moved from Graterford, a dated maximum-security prison in Pennsylvania, to Phoenix, a newly built prison on the same grounds. Before the move, high levels of anxiety and uncertainty prevailed, heightened by the intimidating presence of black-clad special security guards brought in months in advance to facilitate the move. Tension and fear permeated the place.

When the move finally happened, some of the staff, tasked with searching the two boxes of personal possessions each man was allowed to bring with them, vandalized, destroyed, and discarded many items. Religious books, keepsakes, and pictures of family were defaced with sexual, racial, and hateful images and epithets.[5] To make matters worse, the administration initially refused to acknowledge the violations. Even after devising a compensation scheme, there was never an official apology or acknowledgment of wrongdoing, and the perpetrators were never sanctioned.

The bungled move exacerbated the normative level of dignity violations found in prison and left many

71

people traumatized and disillusioned. There were thoughts and even verbalizations of violence and retaliation. Listening justly became a saving grace. The prison was seeded with clusters of trained JL Listeners who were able to visualize an outcome other than violence, mitigate potential escalation, and carry peacefulness with them throughout this time of intense stress and upheaval.

One day, the top brass had come to tour the prison blocks to try to calm the men and assuage fears. But one top official was yelling and visibly irritated because one of the incarcerated men had made an offhand comment that she didn't like. Tension was high. He merely expressed how everyone felt but clearly had touched a nerve. Her voice rose. The strained atmosphere intensified; the potential for violence to erupt was palpable.

The men on the block were agitated and ready to respond in support of this fellow incarcerated person and against the official. In the midst of the rising heat of the moment, one JL Listener felt his "listening training kind of 'kick in.'" He recognized the vulnerability of this person in power and chose to hear her. Turning to her, he calmly and sincerely asked: "It appears as if his comment was a trigger for you?" Seeming to be disarmed by his recognition of her in that heated moment, she looked at the man she had just been yelling at, nodded, excused herself, and walked away instead. Pausing, listening, and responding from a place of genuine care transformed this moment from one of volatility to diffusion.

—JL Listener

Chapter 8
Listening to Our Inner Guidance: Self-Care

All that you touch changes you. All that you change, changes you.

—Octavia Butler

As we engage in self-reflection, identify our listening hurdles, and respond from a place of presence, it might seem like listening is primarily outward-facing or that we do these practices in order to listen justly in an encounter with another. We do. And yet with a listening praxis, we are also listening to and learning about ourselves and hearing the wisdom that arises within us. We have, all along, been increasing our consciousness of our interior worlds. We have been listening inwardly and outwardly in a delicate and beautiful dance; listening is multidirectional.

In this chapter, we delve more deeply into this idea of intentionally listening to ourselves as a matter of self-care. We can care for ourselves before a listening encounter by discerning our capacity to listen healthfully. We can care for ourselves during and after we listen by addressing the potential harm that we can experience when listening to others' pain. We can also develop an ongoing self-care practice of listening to our own inner guidance, attending routinely and consciously to our needs to grieve, heal, celebrate, and thrive. Listening to ourselves is also an act of love, justice, healing, and transformation.

Discerning Our Capacity to Listen with Another

Listening with another person in full presence and attention is no light endeavor, and we are not always in the right frame of heart/mind/body to do so. We are, after all, human. Sometimes we are too ill, wounded, delighted, or otherwise justifiably distracted to be who and what we need to be to listen justly. It is therefore important to take care, pause, and listen to ourselves to discern whether we can begin a listening encounter.

Discernment is thus a key self-care skill. It is the process of finding our own inner wisdom and guidance and, in the case of listening, helps us clarify whether we can engage in a conversation or listening encounter healthfully. We do this with openness and compassion toward ourselves, exploring our own emotions, fears, desires, and patterns and how they impact our ability to listen in that moment. The process thus guides us in making decisions about what is a kind, compassionate, and life-giving response to ourselves and those with whom we listen.

Discernment also helps us to protect ourselves from harm by listening to our bodies, hearts, and minds. How do I feel? Am I in a toxic situation? Do

I need boundaries? Why? Am I safe? Can I listen in this encounter, or is fear or an intervening need blocking me from listening wholeheartedly? It is how we answer questions like:

- What is my best response in this situation?
- What can I freely give and offer in this situation, without resentment, and free of my need to be seen as powerful or a savior?
- What response comes freely from my heart, with no expectation of thanks or recognition from anyone?

Discernment may be clouded by our listening hurdles. With practice, though, we develop the capacity to pause, become present, listen to ourselves, and hear our inner guidance about whether we can listen justly with another person.

Opening to Others' Pain without Harming Ourselves

Listening inevitably opens us to stories of great pain and suffering. Even when our discernment informs us that we are in a healthy frame of heart/mind/body to listen to this pain, it is still important to recognize that we will be impacted by what we hear. Secondary and vicarious trauma, sometimes called compassion fatigue, can not only derail the healing impact of a listening relationship but can be harmful to the listener as well.[1]

> "The expectation that we can be immersed in suffering and loss daily and not be touched by it is as unrealistic as expecting to be able to walk through water without getting wet."
> —Rachel Naomi Remen

These forms of relational exhaustion result from blurry boundaries and an unhealthy egoic focus on ourselves, arising when "we're not hearing the story, we're inserting ourselves into the story."[2] For example, a friend confides that she is trying to leave an abusive partner, and rather than listen, we immediately and physically feel the gravity of the situation and try to fix it. Before honoring our friend's situation by hearing and responding to her story, we begin to make a plan to "rescue" the friend, give unsolicited advice, and make plans to "help" without asking and hearing what our friend sees as her needs and wants. Conversely, healthy boundaries prevent us from getting sucked into unhealthy immersion in other's lives; when someone is drowning, they need a lifeline, not someone in the water drowning with them.

We can safely assume that many of the individuals with whom we interact have suffered heartache or trauma of some form. In order to do no harm in our listening, it is vital that we recognize the prevalence of trauma and the symptoms and behaviors that are its adverse effects. By integrating this trauma-informed awareness into our inner and outer listening, we can not only avoid hooking into someone's trauma-induced pain, but our kind and compassionate listening witness is itself a source of healing.[3]

Only when we are emotionally and physically healthy can we be fully present to the pain, trauma, and suffering of others without taking it on as our own. The first step of such balanced listening is to acknowledge that we are hard wired for empathy and so will be impacted by what we hear. The second is to discern whether we are prepared to listen. If we are, the third step is to listen presently, which entails all of the practices in the preceding chapters but now with an emphasis on self-listening as a way to care for ourselves in the process. Our own thoughts will arise—our to-do list, a memory, a judgment—which we can notice and let go of, returning to presence. But when a thought or physical sensation arises within us that signals a need or concern, we are poised to pay it our attention. Is our heart racing? Are we feeling unsafe? Can we healthfully continue with this conversation? With continued practice, we learn to hear our own needs as they arise, even when immersed in another person's pain.

As a fourth step, we continue the self-care practice of listening to ourselves *after* difficult encounters in order to regulate our own emotions. Unacknowledged, unresolved reactivity and distress can literally make us sick: mentally, emotionally, and physically. This inner work can take many forms, such as meditation, journaling, spiritual practices, or therapy. It may be more listening, rest, boundary-setting, celebration, movement, stillness, or any number of things that lead us to our own unique healing, wholeness, and right relationship with ourselves and others. We can listen to ourselves to learn what form our inner work will take.

Listening to Our Own Needs and Wisdom

The self-care practice of listening to ourselves includes acknowledging that we too have our own histories and stories that need to be articulated and heard. We too have our own inner wisdom and knowing. We can be our own just listeners, letting our sorrows or joys, confusions or clarity arise into our consciousness, where we can attend to them with care.

Not listening and responding to our own needs is endemic. Compassion fatigue and burnout are common, especially among service providers and change agents. Working long hours at multiple jobs creates a life of toxic stress. The twenty-four-hour news cycle and social media can compromise mental health. Imagine trying to listen with someone while struggling with burnout, stress, or depression. It is not easy. Attempting to listen in these states often transfers the very burnout, stress, and depression onto the speaker.

> "One incarcerated Listener was profoundly moved and changed when he decided to practice listening to his inner guidance and connecting to his own goodness. In a rare moment of privacy, he sat quietly on his bed when his cellie was not present. Placing his hand on his chest, he took a breath, focused on himself, and later shared: 'For the first time in seven years, I felt the beating of my own heart.'"
>
> —JL Listener

We cannot truly know our own needs for rest, care, or repair unless we listen to our own bodies, hearts, and minds. Through intentional inner listening, we may notice our listening hurdles that draw our attention away from listening *care*-fully to ourselves. We can notice our wandering minds and return to our inner selves and attend to what resides there. We may witness our own inner critic; here too we simply notice and return to nonjudgmental, compassionate listening to ourselves. We can also respond to ourselves with silent presence, gratitude, affirmation, or with a question, and then keep listening in order to hear our inner responses. This is particularly helpful when we need to make a decision: we can ask ourselves what we truly want, and hear our own voice speak.

Caring for ourselves, including healing our own traumas, creates greater self-awareness, improves our own health, and enhances the quality of our listening presence with others. There is growing recognition that caring for ourselves is a human right and that practicing self-care is a strength, not a weakness. Exercising this right not only benefits ourselves; it also liberates powerful energies that have the potential to transform our relationships and communities.

From Self-Care to Social Transformation

Self-care, and the impact it has on our relationships and listening encounters, is a bridge to social transformation. For example, activist and author Tricia Hersey offers a powerful antidote to capitalism's incessant demands for productivity in her recent book, *Rest is Resistance: A Manifesto,* recasting rest as a radical recalibration of oppressive systems.[4]

Without the self-awareness and intentionality that are the fruit of listening praxis, we reproduce the toxicity of the unjust social systems that exhaust us. It is important that we pause, attune, listen, and then attend to our own mental, physical, spiritual, and relational health in order to offer to ourselves what we wish to bring about in our world. Not only are we worthy of it, we now have clear evidence that support-ing the inner well-being of changemakers is essential for our health and boosts organizational capacity for innovation and collaboration. It ultimately leads to more imaginative, innovative, and effective solutions to social and environmental challenges.[5]

To advocate for and practice intensive self-care is to stand on the threshold of the unknown possibil-ities dwelling within us and lying hidden in every conversation. Our self-listening liberates this latent potential within each of us. With this commitment to listen to and care for ourselves, we can remain com-passionately dedicated to listening for the long haul of peace and justice building.

Self-Care Micro Practices

- Commit to doing your inner work. Be still and notice which inner listening focus discussed in this chapter appeals to you. Pick one or two and stick with them until your inner guidance tells you to try another.
- Listen to yourself every day. Incorporate it in your morning routine and write down your intention to practice throughout the day. At the end of the day, reflect briefly on where

you felt you listened to yourself presently
and without judgment or agenda.

- Practice gratitude. Ask yourself what you are
grateful for and then listen to what arises.
This can be an internal "conversation" or
you can write your question and responses.
Multiple studies have shown that if
repeated for 21 days, this practice lowers
our blood pressure and changes how our
brain perceives the world: we scan our
environments more positively.

- Become conscious of your inner critic and
own self-judgment. Pay attention to how and
when you do this. Change the messaging
by speaking to yourself as you would to a
friend, offering that same compassion to
yourself.

- Keep healthy personal boundaries anchored
in self-awareness and compassion for
yourself and others by asking yourself the
questions on pages 74–75 to determine where
healthy boundaries lie.

- Develop physical, spiritual, or energetic
practices to employ during and after direct
communication with suffering individuals.

- Avoid "picking up" and holding the negative
energies of others. Pray or visualize a "circle
of light" around you that protects you from
and transforms any negative, harmful
energies, but allows love and kindness to
flow in both directions between you and
those you encounter.

- Practice tonglen, also called the "practice of
compassion," whenever you become aware

of suffering or conflict, or during or after challenging encounters. A simple form of this three-breath practice is as follows:

- Breath 1: Take a deep cleansing breath. Open your mind, heart, and body to love and compassionate energies, a Divine Presence/Source Energy . . . whatever works for you. Allow this power to permeate your body as you breathe it in and exhale all negativity, ego, etc. Fill yourself and your heart with this energy.
- Breath 2: Bring awareness to the suffering/conflict you are witnessing. Breathe it into your heart. Feel the texture, the size of your own pain. Allow the suffering of another to enlarge your heart with compassion, but do not embody it. With love and compassion, breathe out healing. It is not necessary to know what form that healing will take. Simply desire and intend it.
- Breath 3: Take one more deep, cleansing breath, intending the healing of yourself and all who suffer. Give thanks.

- When leaving an encounter, bring to mind all that you have experienced. Be aware of where you are carrying any residual tension and anxiety in your body. Intentionally relax these areas and/or engage in a physical activity that releases this tension. Exhale and make a sound, or "shake it off" through your arms, hands, and legs (or whatever physical action works for you).

- Ground yourself. Feel your connection to the earth through your feet, "rooting" yourself in its deep center. Allow any negativity you may be carrying to flow into the earth and be dissolved. Bring the strong, healing energy of Earth up through your feet and let it fill your body. Breathe, breathe, breathe.

STORY

I've been in prison on a wrongful conviction for twenty-six years now. My daughter is twenty-nine years old with two daughters of her own. She doesn't remember me ever being home. To her, without my physical presence, the journey through life has been fatherless. Sometimes when we talk, I mention a memory that I have of us before prison separated us, memories that are full of laughter and times when she felt loved as a child. Those memories remind me of the responsible parent that I had been and allow me to see myself as someone other than the monster that the system projects upon me. I mention the memories to let my daughter know that she hadn't always felt fatherless and that she doesn't have to feel fatherless now.

Unfortunately, my approach has failed to have this desired effect. To her, they are a piercing reminder of my physical absence. Each of the hardships and struggles she's had to endure has become a traumatizing experience that would not have occurred had I been home. Such is the gateway to anger and resentment, which emerges now in most of our

83

conversations. They influence our words and tone of voice and often leave us confused about the love that we clearly share for each other. At times, during our fifteen-minute calls, I seem to be playing defense while she plays offense.

My daughter's hurt has been the hardest reality to prepare for in my upcoming return home, which I hope will be soon. My absence has caused her trauma, I know. How can I not stand in recognition of that? And if it means that I should not mention the memories that I have, then I'll not mention them. But our traumas, hers and mine, would not end there. To not mention these memories disregards my own experience and encourages her to continue looking at our situation through a muddy window, clouded by her pain and the lies about mine. It isn't healing for either of us.

I'm constantly in conversation with myself, working on this, trying to listen without an agenda and bias. It is hard. But I know that as human beings, before we can listen justly to each other, we need to listen to ourselves and explore our own traumas. I am certain that one way or another everyone has trauma to deal with; when we talk to one another, we talk as survivors. If we can master listening to and knowing and understanding ourselves, then listening with and understanding others will be most effective.

I am more open now to respecting boundaries; I don't try to push my agenda with her. I let her know that I love her and keep the window open. And I listen to her, knowing she may need space and time.

—JL Listener

Chapter 9
Listening in Community: Transforming Harm and Doing Justice

Justice is what love looks like in public.

—Cornel West

As a young boy in the mid-nineteenth century, *Alaxchiiaahush*, also known as Plenty-coups, the last traditional tribal chief of the Crow (*Apsaalooké*) Nation, had a powerful dream that featured a tiny chickadee, known to the crow as the bird who listens, learns, and adapts.[1] The dream was interpreted by tribal elders to foretell the end of the buffalo, the survival of the Crow, and the necessity of learning from the chickadee as this massive shift occurred. What the dream ultimately meant to the Crow nation can only be known and expressed by a tribal member. But what can be said is that at a time of chaos, social disintegration, and culture-collapse, a group of traumatized and dispirited people took guidance and derived hope from a fellow creature, the chickadee, whose survival is dependent upon listening and adapting.

We recognize this wisdom from the Crow as wisdom for our current times of social and cultural upheaval and discord and note that we too must listen and adapt. We do not change indiscriminately; we listen, like the chickadee, and are willing to be changed by what we hear.

While the listening values and practices offered in the preceding chapters can apply to any interaction that we might have in our daily lives, we can also apply them with specific intent to respond to discord and rupture. We can listen and adapt to what arises when we make intentional space to attend to interpersonal and systemic harms in our communities. This chapter turns to this relationship between listening and the formal and informal ways in which we do the work of transforming harm and doing justice between and among us.

Formal Processes for Transforming Harm

Mediation

Listening is the heart of mediation. Mediation is a structured, supportive process in which a neutral third party assists disputing parties in constructively resolving their disagreements. It involves clarifying misunderstandings, identifying concerns, finding areas of accord, and honoring the dignity of all parties in the process of reaching mutually agreeable solutions. Many forms of mediation consist of a series of listening sessions, beginning with separate preparatory conversations with the disputing parties, as well as other stakeholders. Careful listening at this point surfaces the unique information needed to understand the conflict and customize the process, before bringing people together.

Listening is equally important during the mediation itself, and mediators can help ground the process by guiding participants with listening values and praxis. Everyone present must be able to hear what is being said and, though the objective is often a written agreement between parties, it can be powerful, for example, to listen without a specific agenda and with radical humility and curiosity throughout the process, especially when disputes are born of deep resentments. After an agreement is reached, participants are able to adapt to its parameters if it is the product of such a mutually dignifying undertaking.

Restorative Justice

Restorative justice (RJ) is a philosophy and set of practices designed to prevent and respond to harm and intentionally build community and connection through dialogue processes, such as circles and conferencing. Commonly used in situations of criminal harm, school-based harm, and increasingly in community settings, these practices bring together multiple stakeholders, including the person who was harmed, the person who caused the harm, their supporters, and community members. Together, with the assistance of a facilitator (or keeper, in the case of circles), they identify the harm(s), its impacts, and the needs that have arisen, and then collectively decide, when appropriate, what accountability and "putting right" can mean for all involved.

Listening in these contexts is perhaps most vital yet can be extremely challenging when dialogue participants have experienced trauma, especially in situations of severe or fatal violence. Experiencing or perpetrating such harm can lead to a loss of meaning or put one out of touch with themselves and their innate sense of dignity and worth. Before being able to listen to another, participants need to be afforded the opportunity to listen to their own internal voice, to the meaning-making and dignity-repairing stories that arise within them. To participate in the deeply vulnerable practice of a restorative justice dialogue, for example, participants need assurance that they will be listened to and be given the time and space to practice listening to another person in the fullness of their humanity.

Listening praxis on the part of the facilitator/keeper is therefore an integral part of preparing participants for a restorative encounter and facilitating or keeping the process. As they model listening, participants can learn to listen to themselves and each other.

Listening within the broader field of RJ is also critical as scholars and practitioners of color in the United States and beyond raise important questions about professionalization; diversity, equity, and inclusion; and whether the social-systemic "first harm" of the genocide of Native peoples and the "second harm" of chattel slavery are adequately addressed when attending to interpersonal harms within restorative practices. *Colorizing Restorative Justice* is a recent anthology that voices such concerns that need to be heard in order for the field to honor its indigenous roots and the social systemic harms that are perpetuated if not made visible in the practices.[2]

Transformative Justice

Transformative justice (TJ) is a variety of movements, theories, and practices to transform interpersonal harm (including criminal harm) within communities, often explicitly without the use of the criminal justice system, while simultaneously calling attention and attempting to change the systemic injustices within which interpersonal harms occur.

TJ has multiple origins and contemporary iterations. One historical thread is the millennia of indigenous practices that have always been considered transformative and are distinct from (yet inform) the contemporary global RJ movement. Another historical thread has TJ originating among poor women and transwomen of color in the United States in the early 2000s as they addressed conflict—sometimes violent conflict—in their communities without being able to trust the criminal justice system that otherwise criminalized them.[3] It is therefore a movement born of pure necessity to fill the gaps created by the criminal justice system.

This latter branch of TJ takes an explicit abolitionist stance against the prison industrial complex and places survivor safety, accountability, and transformation of the social conditions that produce violence at the center of its work. Generally, TJ movements prefer to transform conflict and harm by addressing interpersonal harm within the context of addressing larger, social-systemic harms at the same time, noting that for poor and over-policed communities that are plagued by violence, including police violence, the goal should not be to *restore* justice, since there was no justice initially, but to transform the systemic conditions that produce interpersonal harms within such communities.[4]

One TJ practice, called a community accountability circle, brings stakeholders in the community together to respond to harm. Like RJ, listening is critical for this TJ practice. Participants not only have to deal with interpersonal harm(s) but also with the pain of being traumatized by myriad social systems and institutions that marginalize and oppress, instead of offering the social support that they purport to provide. The TJ facilitator listens attentively and provides structure amidst these complex emotions, guiding participants as they collectively work toward safety, healing, justice, and community account-ability. Transformative justice activists Mariame Kaba and Shira Hassan emphasize the importance of listening in their TJ workbook, *Fumbling Towards Repair*. They note that listening well on the part of the coordinator or facilitator and participants in a community accountability circle includes attention, withholding judgment, openness, and caring.

Listening and Living in Right Relationship

Some of the formal processes above draw from the practices of indigenous people, for whom peace-making is a way of life. For example, in the Navajo nation, the phrase describing this process is *hozhooji naat'aanii*, loosely translated as peacemaking; the word really means something more like "people talking together to re-form relationships with each other and the universe." The process includes the concept of *k'e*, or respect, which means "to restore my dignity, to restore my worthiness." Disputes are resolved not by laws or on behalf of a state but by the building and rebuilding of community and relation-ships.[5] This is accomplished by having all parties and affected community members listen to each other from a place of deep mutuality and belonging.

For many indigenous groups, peacemaking is not a set-aside, formal practice but a way of being, an integral part of living with a keen awareness of our interconnectedness with each other and the natural world and the need for harmony.

Howard Zehr invites all of us to a similar way of being through his "10 Ways to Live Restoratively." The seventh recommendation mentions listening explicitly:

"Listen, deeply and compassionately, to others, seeking to understand, even if you don't agree with them. (Think about who you want to be rather than just being right.)"

The parenthetical note prompts us to think consciously about why we are listening and what preconceived outcome we might have in mind. Though not mentioned explicitly, listening is actually vital to each and every one of these ways to live restoratively.[6] By prioritizing listening in daily life, we potentially harm less, so that there becomes less need for the practices of addressing harm and conflict. Listening midwifes the potential for a new way of being and doing justice in every interaction.

Kaba and Hassan also invite us to consider living in a way that reduces harm in addition to having formal practices. One of the frameworks that guides their transformative justice work is harm reduction, which they refer to as "a philosophy of living, surviving, and resisting oppression and violence that centers self-determination and non-condemning access to an array of options . . . [and] is the union of healing and community-building at its finest." This too requires listening in order to meet people exactly where they are.[7]

91

Taken together, all of the approaches described above are tipping the scales of justice toward a transformation of current methods of repairing harm. Listening is essential to this process and accelerates the pace of this desperately needed shift.

Micro Practices for Transforming Harm and Doing Justice

- Become familiar with the history and contemporary contributions of the indigenous people who occupied/still live on the land where you live. Listen to their stories.
- Learn about land acknowledgments and which organizations/institutions where you work or live use them in a meaningful way. Encourage those who don't to engage in meaningful conversations to consider adopting one; this can be done in cooperation with local indigenous groups.
- Learn about systemic oppressions and your place within the social hierarchies of your society; listen to people's stories of systemic oppression and resilience. Listen to the histories and contributions of descendants of previously enslaved people, of people from colonized places.
- Listen to/learn about the peacemaking processes of your own ancestors as well as people from different cultural backgrounds than you.
- Practice Howard Zehr's "10 ways to live restoratively" (the full list is on pages 105-106).

- Think about ways in which you have caused harm; if given the opportunity, listen to the ways in which your words or actions impacted someone and how that harm might be repaired.
- In a supported way, think about a harm you have experienced; imagine listening to the person who harmed you take accountability for that harm. If safe to do so, reach out to that person to talk about the experience and repair the harm.
- Volunteer with a local mediation, restorative, or transformative justice program.
- Become trained in dialogue facilitation in its many forms.
- Join community dialogic efforts to address community violence, such as police and gun violence; violence perpetrated by hate groups; violence and oppression against any marginalized group of people.
- Practice just listening as a way of life.

STORY

A few years back, I served as a juror. It was immediately clear when the jury began deliberating that we had a problem: the majority were in agreement on how to move forward but two jurors vehemently disagreed. We made no progress after an entire afternoon and returned the next morning. The debate turned ugly and dissolved into heated arguments with name-calling and tears. At one point, the two individuals who disagreed with the group turned their chairs so that their backs were facing us. The discussion abruptly ended. The deputy begged us to work together and come to a compromise. He reminded us that, if we did not, we would have to spend the entire next day back in that room and possibly after the weekend. He suggested we take a lunch break and try to relax.

No one spoke as he brought the pizza to our table. I was feeling the stress and tension in my entire body. I could barely chew my food. As I sat at the table, my eyes glanced around the room at each person, including the two with their backs to us eating pizza on their laps so they wouldn't have to look at us.

I wondered what listening skill I could choose to open some doors and break through the anger. Curiosity was the first thing that came to mind. I began by asking the foreman to tell us a little about himself. He was stiff at first, still angry, but gracious enough to share. Each person shared a little about themselves with the group, and one of the jurors with their back turned to the table slowly inched their chair around. When it was their turn to speak, they said to me, "What do you do?" I briefly shared about my family and about Just Listening and its volunteer projects. When I mentioned our prison project, they both became intrigued and turned their chairs back to the table, peppering me with questions. "Why do you go there?" "Aren't you afraid?"

I shared a story about a man who had developed a relationship with his victim's family who had won a civil suit and was receiving all monies the man earned as part of the court decision. After serving his time, he was released and went home to his family. Heartbreakingly, one week later his adult son was murdered; he was devastated with no money to bury him. His victim's family learned of this and went to the man, giving him the money he needed to provide his son with a proper burial. By the time I had finished my story, the woman had tears in her eyes. Suddenly, we were having a conversation about forgiveness, love, and goodness.

Tension was dissipating and hearts had softened. Our foreman gently leaned on the table and suggested we try to come to a compromise. Within an hour and a half we had one, called our deputy in, and told him we were ready to go back into the courtroom.

—JL Listener

Chapter 10
Listening and Possibility: The Transformed World

Transform yourself to transform the world.
—Grace Lee Boggs

Listening justly carries the potential to impact ourselves, others, and communities. It builds belonging and safety, transforms conflicts, bridges divides, heals harms, and opens possibilities for peace between and among people and with our natural world. Listening also makes it possible to transform whole cultures, societies, and the world to ones characterized by love, justice, compassion, and equity.[1] Developing just listening habits launches change; embodying them initiates transformation.

We and our planet home are in crisis as our social systems, institutions, and the earth itself undergo seismic shifts and what feels like chaos and instability—e.g., poverty, racism, climate change, and human violence. This has created historic levels of fear, social isolation, loneliness, and despair. We ache for a world where people and living systems are valued

over profit, and the well-being of the whole is priori-
tized over the inequitable advantage of the few. These
problems are human made; they originated in our
thoughts and beliefs and have been carried out in our
collective activities. We have created them.

We can therefore create them differently. We
can create a just and equitable world where all life
thrives in balance and harmony and where all are
accountable, take responsibility, and center the common good. We can build a better world where all
are housed, fed, educated, cared for, loved, provided
health care, and paid just wages for meaningful
work. Where war and gun violence are no more.
Where humans honor and acknowledge our interconnectedness with all life. A world in which we listen
to those of us who have little to no recognized power
and, in doing so, reallocate and shift the very definition of power and balance power with marginalized
communities.[2]

Social transformation requires a bottom-up
approach, beginning with individual transformation that yields collective transformation, and then
expands. Change comes from the margins. Each
of us can assume leadership in accomplishing this
change by choosing to listen justly every day in every
encounter. We can pause, be present, and notice and
respond to what emerges as current needs, solutions,
possibilities, and creativity. The generative nature of
listening transforms.

Promising Shifts
There is evidence of individual and communal shifts
toward more just relationships erupting throughout
the world, efforts which are gaining momentum,

supported by focused research and philanthropic interest.[3]

We can look to individuals whose personal journeys of transformation have led to change that reverberates throughout their communities and into the wider world. Oscar Romero in El Salvador. Wangari Maathai, Kenyan founder of the environmental Green Belt Movement. Former white nationalist and supremacist Derek Black. Former neo-Nazi Shannon Martinez. Former jihadist Jesse Morton. All of these individuals—to name only a few—were nurtured by compassionate relationships with others, characterized by mutual listening. They listened to the emerging wisdom of their own hearts, the needs and longings of their communities, and then shared those insights with others in ways that are transforming the systems and institutions in which they were immersed.

This recognition of the need to listen to all voices and to embrace listening values has also found expression in the organizational structures of many groups and nascent movements globally. Entities of all kinds—from small public benefit organizations to corporations—are experimenting with emergent insights and methods of organizational change, and creating work environments characterized by listening and listening values, such as cooperation, love, community, and justice.[4] Movements such as Black Lives Matter, #MeToo, the Occupy Movement, Community Courts, Integrative Community Therapy in Brazil and now the United States, and cross-sector partnerships center listening to all voices as a core practice.

Individuals and groups around the globe are recognizing and valuing the ancient insights and practices of indigenous people, who have listened to and learned from all of nature for millennia. Such listening reveals that all beings thrive when cooperation and the good of all are employed as operating principles.[5]

Listening justly accelerates these individual, collective, and cultural shifts and is potentially transformative in any place or circumstance where human dignity is violated, whether interpersonally or communally,[6] even in prison, an inherently tense, violent, and traumatizing environment. In these promising shifts, we can sense the as-yet-unimagined world of justice and peace that we can produce by listening together.

Becoming Butterflies and Trim Tabs

We are building a web of connection. I see growing connectivity: language changes, increased social and community cohesion, networks linking up. There is growing recognition that all voices need to be heard. We need to intentionally and purposefully listen to each other.

—Prabha Sankanarayan

We might draw further wisdom and guidance for how to bring about a just and equitable world by listening to the natural world. For example, evolutionary biologists have long noted the natural process of transformation when a caterpillar enters the chrysalis and becomes a butterfly. Hidden within the disintegrating body of the caterpillar are structures called imaginal discs, which are activated as the process of becoming a butterfly progresses.

When the disks mature and become imaginal cells, they form themselves into a new pattern, thus transforming the disintegrating body of the caterpillar into the butterfly. The breakdown of the caterpillar's old system is essential for the breakthrough of the new butterfly. Yet, the caterpillar neither dies nor disintegrates, for from the beginning its hidden purpose was to transform and be reborn as the butterfly.[7]

We humans and our social systems are both disintegrating bodies and imaginal cells, not yet aware of what we might be. Listening is an essential element of transforming and being reborn as new people who can imagine a new, just, and equitable world. It is hard to imagine what is not already here, something new rather than a reform of what currently is. But it is possible. We can be different. Our world can be transformed beyond what we think we already know.

To do this, we begin with ourselves. Personal transformation occurs when we engage in inner listening and abandon old patterns of blame, judgment, fear, and reactivity. We arrive at a place of inner coherence and resonance: we learn to be present and listen in all social relationships and spaces. Only then can we be sources of love, justice, healing, and transformation and activate our imagination and that of others.

Collective, large-scale transformation happens when a sufficient number of human "imaginal cells"— people engaged in the same conscious imagining— link up in community and consciousness and become "saturated in qualities of love, gratefulness, generosity, and compassion."[8] In this way, listening justly is a trim tab,[9] a small intervention that yields massive results. We can all be trim tabs, tiny mediators of transformative change, wherever we find ourselves.

Invoking our imaginations and living in the possibility of a new, just world allows transformation to unfold. We activate the vast resource of our imaginations and as-yet-undreamed possibilities, solutions, and resources through practice, until our imagination, so integral to our humanity, is regularly accessed and expressed.

The temptation to declare a shift to this new world impossible, to dally with despair, is understandable as we slog through the injustice and divisions at every level of our fragile social order. But radical listening is the antidote: the unimagined-solutions that we need lie not within one person or viewpoint, but in our collective minds, hearts, and imaginations. Not only do each of us hold the solutions to our own issues within, but together, we hold the vision and transformative capacities for humanity.[10]

Justice, Healing, Transformation . . . and Love

Each listening interaction holds the potential of healing, restoration, and transformation. The work of transforming ourselves and the world by adopting a listening praxis is not flashy; it requires only two ears, courage, an open heart, caring people, and a willingness to take the time needed to build relationships.

We can listen as a radical act of love, justice, healing, and transformation. But the fiery core is love. All things are mended and transformed by love: it is the most powerful force in the universe, a quantum power of infinite and unknowable potential, without conditions and limitations.

Working together on this project has itself been the practice of listening justly. This collaboration has been life-affirming and sustaining; it has deepened our relationships, bonded us as community, and strengthened our commitment to living lives of love, justice, healing, and transformation. Although we are many, it is one heart that animates this book. Together, we have created something new that we had not imagined alone.

The journey of justice and social change is challenging and potentially disheartening: embracing this listening praxis is itself the change, and transformative. Let's travel this path together, with relentless compassion and radical humility, just listening all the way.

10 Ways to Live Restoratively

Howard Zehr

1. Take relationships seriously, envisioning yourself in an interconnected web of people, institutions, and the environment.
2. Try to be aware of the impact—potential as well as actual—of your actions on others and the environment.
3. When your actions negatively impact others, take responsibility by acknowledging and seeking to repair the harm—even when you could probably get away with avoiding or denying it.
4. Treat everyone respectfully, even those you don't expect to encounter again, even those you feel don't deserve it, even those who have harmed or offended you or others.
5. Involve those affected by a decision, as much as possible, in the decision-making process.
6. View the conflicts and harms in your life as opportunities.

7. Listen, deeply and compassionately, to others, seeking to understand, even if you don't agree with them. (Think about who you want to be rather than just being right.)
8. Engage in dialogue with others, even when what is being said is difficult, remaining open to learning from them and the encounter.
9. Be cautious about imposing your "truths" and views on other people and situations.
10. Sensitively confront everyday injustices including sexism, racism, homophobia, and classism.

Suggested Resources

For an extensive, periodically updated resource list and study guide, see http://justlistening.net/the-little-book -of-JUST-listening/

For those readers unable to access the internet, please send a request for the Study Guide and/ or Resource List to: JUST Listening, 26 W. Gowen Avenue, Philadelphia, PA 19119.

Community and Connection

Block, Peter. (2018). *Community: The Structure of Belonging* (2nd ed.). Berrett-Koehler Publishers.

Brown, Brené. (2021) *Atlas of the Heart: Mapping Meaningful Connection and the Language of Human Experience.* Random House.

hooks, bell. (2003). *Teaching Community: A Pedagogy of Hope* (1st ed.). Routledge.

Listening

Lindahl, Kay. (2001). *The Sacred Art of Listening: Forty Reflections for Cultivating a Spiritual Practice, SkyLight Paths.*

Murphy, Kate. (2020). *You're Not Listening: What You're Missing and Why It Matters* (Reprint). Celadon Books.

Peavey, Fran (2019) *Strategic Questioning Manual: A Powerful Tool for Personal and Social Change.* The Commons Social Change Library. https://commonslibrary.org/strategic-questioning/#:~:text = Strategic%20questioning%20is%20an%20 approach,strategies%20and%20ideas%20for%20 change.

Shafir, Rebecca. (2003). *The Zen of Listening: Mindful Communication in the Age of Distraction* (New edition). Quest Books.

Miscellaneous

Banaji, Mahzarin, and Anthony Greenwald. (2016). *Blindspot: Hidden Biases of Good People* (Reprint). Random House Publishing Group.

Restorative and Transformative Justice

Kaba, Mariame, and Shira Hassan (2019). *Fumbling Towards Repair: A Workbook for Community Accountability Facilitators.* Project NIA and Justice Practice.

Kimmerer, Robin. W. (2015). *Braiding Sweetgrass: Indigenous Wisdom, Scientific Knowledge and the Teachings of Plants* (First Paperback). Milkweed Editions.

Valandra, Edward C. (Waŋbli Waphấha Hokšíla) (ed.). (2020) *Colorizing Restorative Justice: Voicing Our Realities.* Living Justice Press.

Social Change and Transformation

Bridle, James. (2022). *Ways of Being: Animals, Plants, Machines: The Search for a Planetary Intelligence.* Farrar, Straus, and Giroux.

brown, adrienne maree. (2017). *Emergent Strategy: Shaping Change, Changing Worlds (Emergent Strategy, 0)* (Reprint). AK Press.

Hersey, Tricia. (2022). *Rest Is Resistance: A Manifesto.* Little, Brown Spark.

Wheatley, Margaret J. (2023). *Who Do We Choose to Be? Facing Reality. Claiming Leadership, Restoring Sanity, Second Edition.* Oakland, CA. Berrett-Koehler Publishers, Inc.

Trauma

Menachem, Resmaa. (2017) *My Grandmother's Hands: Racialized Trauma and the Pathway to Mending Our Hearts and Bodies.* Central Recovery Press.

Van der Kolk, Bessel. (2015). *The Body Keeps the Score: Brain, Mind, and Body in the Healing of Trauma.* Penguin Publishing Group.

Contributors

The following Listeners have contributed material for this book.

Bruce Bainbridge
Charles Bassett
Sharon Browning
Eric Burley
Carl Cooper
Joe Callan
Mary Callan
Bernadette M. Cronin-Geller
Donna Duffey
Lisa Feix
Kathy Flaherty
Terrance Graham
Peter Hogan
Fred Magondu
Catherine Mannion
Brenna McGinnis
Judy Miller
Kenneth Miller
Kevin Mines
JoLynn Mokos
Yahya John Moore
Zach Nichols

Frank Palmieri
Meredith Penn
Paul Perry
Felix Rosado
Ella Rose
Kareem Sampson
Virgil Shaw
Larry Stephenson
Larry Stromberg
Tricia Way
Floyd Wilson
Andre Wright
Diane Zeig

Endnotes

Chapter 1

1 Martin Luther King, Jr., "Where Do We Go from Here?," (speech), August 16, 1967, Southern Christian Leadership Conference, Atlanta, Georgia. YouTube, Uploaded by CDBaby, 11/14/15. https://www.youtube.com/watch?v = 3e0C5rXAjfM.

2 Dalai Lama and Desmond Tutu. 2016. *The Book of Joy: Lasting Happiness in a Changing World.* New York, Avery. ix.

Chapter 2

1 For resources to address this, see "The Trust Network Resource Library," Trust Network, https://www.the trustnetwork.net/resource-library#search-the -library.

2 The work of John T. Cacioppo is helpful. For a quick overview, see John Cacioppo, "The Lethality of Loneliness," September 9, 2013, TEDx Des Moines, TED video, 18:44, https://www.youtube .com/watch?v = _0hxl03JoA0. See also Brené Brown, *Atlas of the Heart: Mapping Meaningful Connection and the Language of Human Experience* (New York: Random House, 2021), 179; Julianne Holt-Lunstad, Timothy B. Smith, and J. Bradley Layton,

"Social Relationships and Mortality Risk: A Meta-Analytic Review,". *PLoS Medicine* 7, no. 7 (2010): 1–20, quoted in Brown, *Atlas of the Heart*, 180.

3   Bethany Rittle-Johnson, Megan Saylor, and Kathryn E. Swygert, "Learning from Explaining: Does It Matter If mom Is Listening?," *Journal of Experimental Child Psychology* 100, no. 3 (July 2008): 215–24, https://doi.org/10.1016/j.jecp.2007.10.002; Robert M. Krauss, "The Role of the Listener: Addressee Influences on Message Formulation," *Journal of Language and Social Psychology* 6, no. 2 (June 1987): 81–98, https://doi.org/10.1177/0261927X8700600201; Kate Loewenthal, "The Development of Codes in Public and Private Language," Psychonomic Science 8, (1967): 449–50. https://doi.org/10.3758/BF03332285, quoted in Kate Murphy, *You're Not Listening: What You're Missing and Why It Matters* (New York: Celadon Books, 2019), 148. Center For Addiction and Mental Health, "Stress," CAMH (website), n.d., https://www.camh.ca/en/health-info/mental-illness-and-addiction-index/stress#:~:text=When%20stress%20becomes%20overwhelming%20and,complaints%20such%20as%20muscle%20tension. For information on grief, see Francis Weller, *The Wild Edge of Sorrow* (Berkeley, CA: North Atlantic Books, 2015). For dealing with trauma, see Evelyn Jaffe Schrieber, ed., *Healing Trauma: The Power of Listening* (New York: International Psychoanalytic Books, 2015).

4   Daniel Siegle, *The Developing Mind: Toward a Neurobiology of Interpersonal Experience* (New York: Guilford Press, 1999); Mark Brady, "Why Your Story One-Upping My Story Is Bad for My Brain . . . and Yours," *Flowering Brain* (blog),

April 26, 2015, https://floweringbrain.wordpress
.com/2015/04/26/why-your-story-one-upping-my-
story-is-bad-for-my-brain-and-yours/.

5   Jonas T. Kaplan, Sarah I. Gimbel, and Sam
    Harris, "Neural Correlates of Maintaining One's
    Political Beliefs in the Face of Counterevidence,"
    Scientific Reports 6 (December 2016): https://doi
    .org/10.1038/srep39589.

6   Kenneth Cloke, "Bringing Oxytocin into the Room:
    Notes on the Neurophysiology of Conflict," Mediate
    .com, January 19, 2009, https://mediate.com/bringing
    -oxytocin-into-the-room-notes-on-the-neurophysi
    ology-of-conflict/.

7   James Bridle, *Ways of Being: Animals, Plants,
    Machines: The Search for a Planetary Intelligence*
    (New York: Picador, 2022), 17. David Abram ini-
    tiated the use of the term *more-than-human world*
    to shift our human tendency to separate ourselves
    from the natural world. This term includes "every
    inhabitant of the biosphere . . . the animals,
    plants, bacteria, fungi and viruses. It includes the
    rivers, seas, winds, stones, and clouds that sup-
    port, shake, and shadow us."

8   Linda Bell Grdina, Nora Johnson, and Aaron
    Pereira, "Connecting Individual and Societal
    Change," *Stanford Social Innovation Review* (2020):
    https://doi.org/10.48558/A67W-CT94.

9   Derrick Jensen, *A Language Older Than Words*
    (White River Junction, VT: Chelsea Green
    Publishing Company, 2000), 372.

Chapter 3

1   Nick Obelensky, *Complex Adaptive Leadership:
    Embracing Paradox and Uncertainty* (Burlington,

VT: Gower, 2014), as quoted in adrienne maree brown, *Emergent Strategy: Shaping Change, Changing Worlds.* (Chico, CA: AK Press, 2017), 3.

2 Fred Magondu, "Dignity and Restorative Justice," Internet Journal of Restorative Justice (website), August 2021, https://www.rj4allpublications.com/product/dignity-and-restorative-justice/.

3 Danielle Sered, *Until We Reckon* (New York: New Press, 2021), 14.

4 Brown, *Atlas of the Heart*, 123.

5 See the work of Emile Bruneau, e.g. Emile G. Bruneau, Rebecca Saxe. "The power of being heard: The benefits of 'perspective-giving' in the context of intergroup conflict," *Journal of Experimental Social Psychology* 48, no. 4, 2012, Pages 855–866, https://doi.org/10.1016/j.jesp.2012.02.017.

EG Bruneau, M Cikara, R Saxe. "Parochial empathy predicts reduced altruism and the endorsement of passive harm." *Social Psychological and Personality Science*, 2017.

Emile: The Mission of Emile Bruneau of the Peace and Conflict Neuroscience Lab, 2021. Annenberg School for Communication, YouTube video. https://www.youtube.com/watch?v=kJvfqft5v9U.

6 Peter Block, *Community: The Structure of Belonging* (Oakland, CA: Berret-Koehler Publishers, 2018), 1, 190.

Chapter 4

1 Paulo Freire, *Pedagogy of the Oppressed* (New York: Seabury Press, 1970), 5.

Chapter 5

1   For greater details, see the many books and articles of Deborah Tannen; Cloke, "Bringing Oxytocin into the Room"; Helen Riess, "The Science of Empathy," *Journal of Patient Experience* 4 no. 2 (2017): 74–77, https://doi:10.1177/2374373517699267; Vilayanur Ramachadran, "The Neurons That Shaped Civilization," 2009, TEDIndia, TED video, 7:27, https://www.ted.com/talks/vilayanur_ramachandran_the_neurons_that_shaped_civilization?language = en.

2   *Cellie* is slang for a prison cellmate in many prison settings.

Chapter 6

1   Shankar Vedantam, "Mind of the Village: Understanding Our Implicit Biases," *Hidden Brain*, June 20, 2020, radio broadcast, text and audio, 50:30, https://www.npr.org/2020/06/20/880379282/the-mind-of-the-village-understanding-our-implicit-biases.

2   Sara Konrath, Edward O'Brien, and Courtney Hsing. May 2011. "Changes in Dispositional Empathy in American College Students over Time: A Meta-Analysis," *Personality and Social Psychology Review* 15(2):180–98.

3   M. Kingwell, *Unruly Voices: Essays on Democracy, Civility and the Human Imagination* (Ontario: Biblioasis, 17), quoted in World Economic Forum, *The Global Risks Report 2019* (Geneva: World Economic Forum, 2019), 41, https://www3.weforum.org/docs/WEF_Global_Risks_Report_2019.pdf.

4   This study found that only 2.5 percent of humans are capable of effective multitasking: Jason M.

Watson and David L. Strayer, "Supertaskers: Profiles in Extraordinary Multitasking Ability," *Psychonomic Bulletin & Review* 17 (2010): 479–85, https://doi.org/10.3758/PBR.17.4.479. See also Murphy, *You're Not Listening*, 261.

5   Gloria Mark, Daniela Gudith, and Ulrich Klocke, "The Cost of Interrupted Work: More Speed and Stress," *Proceedings of the Conference on Human Factors in Computing Systems* (April 2008): 107–10, https://doi.org/10.1145/1357054.1357072.

6   Stefan Tams et al., "Grappling with Modern Technology: Interruptions Mediated by Mobile Devices Impact Older Workers Disproportionately," *Information Systems and E-Business Management* 20 (2022): 635–55, https://doi.org/10.1007/s10257-021-00526-3; Brandon T. McDaniel, "Parent Distraction with Phones, Reasons for Use, and Impacts on Parenting and Child Outcomes: A Review of the Emerging Research," *Human Behavior and Emerging Technologies* 1, no. 2 (April 2019): 69–175, https://doi.org/10.1002/hbe2.139;

"The Impact of Interruptions," Berkeley People & Culture, University of California Berkeley, n.d., https://hr.berkeley.edu/impact-interruptions.

7   Julie Tseng and Jordan Poppenk, "Brain Meta-State Transitions Demarcate Thoughts across Task Contexts Exposing the Mental Noise of Trait Neuroticism," *Nature Communications* 11 (2020): https://doi.org/10.1038/s41467-020-17255-9.

8   Matthew A. Killingsworth and Daniel T. Gilbert, "A Wandering Mind Is an Unhappy Mind," *Science* 330, no. 6006 (November 12, 2010): 932, https://doi.org/10.1126/science.1192439.

9   The information and perspectives in this section are derived from Eckhart Tolle's full and insightful discussion of ego: Eckhart Tolle, *A New Earth* (New York, Penguin, 2005), especially chapter 3.

10 Don H. Zimmermann and Candace West, "Sex Roles, Interruptions and Silences in Conversation. In *Amsterdam Studies in the Theory and History of Linguistic Science*, vol. 4, ed. Konrad Koerner (Amsterdam: John Benjamins, 1996), 211–36; Helen Riess, "The Science of Empathy," *Journal of Patient Experience* 4, no. 2 (June 2017): 74–77, https://doi.org/10.1177/2374373517699267; Charles Derber, *The Pursuit of Attention: Power and Ego in Everyday Life,* 2nd ed. (London: Oxford University Press, 2000).

11 Deborah Gray White, *Ar'n't I a Woman?: Female Slaves in the Plantation South* (New York: W. W. Norton, 1999);
    Daphna Motro et al., "The 'Angry Black Woman' Stereotype at Work," *Harvard Business Review*, January 31, 2022, https://hbr.org/2022/01/the-angry-black-woman-stereotype-at-work.

12 Mahzarin R. Banaji and Anthony Greenwald, *Blind Spot: Hidden Biases of Good People* (New York: Bantam Books, 2016).

13 Susan Cain, *Quiet: The Power of Introverts in a World That Won't Stop Talking* (New York: Crown Publishing, 2013).

14 For a more comprehensive list of commonly used violent terms, see "Violent Phrases That Are Used in Everyday Speech," Center for Hope & Safety, n.d., https://hopeandsafety.org/learn-more/violent-language/. For suggestions of alternative terms and phrasing, see Elizabeth Grim, "Adopting

Inclusive and Non-Violent Language: Part 2," Elizabeth Grim Consulting, March 17, 2021, https://elizabethgrim.com/adopting-inclusive-and-non-violent-language-part-2/.

Chapter 7

1 Fran Peavey, *Strategic Questioning Manual: A Powerful Tool for Personal and Social Change* (Melbourne: The Commons Social Change Library, n.d.), https://commonslibrary.org/strategic-questioning.
2 Brené Brown, "Brené Brown on Empathy vs. Sympathy," YouTube video, 2:53, https://www.youtube.com/watch?v=KZBTYViDPlQ.
3 Parker Palmer, *A Hidden Wholeness: The Journey Toward an Undivided Life* (San Francisco: Jossey-Bass, 2009).
4 Bernard Lee, "Rules for A Dialogic Community" (lecture, ForMission, Religious Formation Conference, Oblate School of Theology, San Antonio, TX, Spring 2004, quoted in Annmarie Sanders, *However Long the Night: Making Meaning in a Time of Crisis: A Spiritual Journey of the Leadership Conference of Women Religious* (self-pub., CreateSpace Independent Publishing Platform, 2018), 58–59.
5 Samantha Melamed, "Inmates Allege 'Hate Crimes' by Staff at SCI Phoenix, Pennsylvania's Newest Prison," *Philadelphia Inquirer*, September 4, 2018, https://www.inquirer.com/philly/news/pennsylvania-prison-strike-sci-phoenix-graterford-department-of-corrections-20180904.html.

Chapter 8

1 Rose M. Perrine, "On Being Supportive: The Emotional Consequences of Listening to

Another's Distress," *Journal of Social and Personal Relationships* 10, no. 3 (1993): 371–84, https://doi .org/10.1177/0265407593103005; Tzvi Michelson and Avraham Kluger, "Can Listening Hurt You? A Meta-Analysis of the Effects of Exposure to Trauma on Listener's Stress, *International Journal of Listening* 37, no. 1 (2023): https://doi.org/10.108 0/10904018.2021.1927734.

2   Brown, *Atlas of the Heart,* 125.

3   Bessel van der Kolk, *The Body Keeps the Score: Brain, Mind, and Body in the Healing of Trauma* (London: Penguin Books, 2015).

4   Grdina, Johnson, and Pereira, "Connecting Individual and Societal Change."

5   Ibid.

Chapter 9

1   This dream is recounted in detail in Linderman, Frank Bird. Plenty-coups: *Chief of the Crows,* (Lincoln: University of Nebraska Press, 2002) (originally published January 1, 1890), and its implications for a time of collapse are discussed extensively in Jonathan Lear, *Radical Hope: Ethics in the Face of Cultural Devastation* (Cambridge, MA: Harvard University Press, 2008).

2   Edward C. Valandra and Waŋbli Wapȟáha Hokšíla, eds., *Colorizing Restorative Justice: Voicing Our Realities* (Saint Paul, MN: Living Justice Press, 2020).

3   Miriam Kaba and Shira Hassan, *Fumbling Towards Repair: A Workbook for Community Accountability Facilitators* (Chico, CA: AK Press, 2019).

4   For deeper exploration of these conversations, see Kaba and Hassan, *Fumbling Towards Repair* and

M. Kay Harris, "Transformative Justice," chap. 38 in *Handbook of Restorative Justice: A Global Perspective*, ed. Dennis Sulivan and Larry Tifft (London: Routlege, 2007).

5   Robert Yazzie and James Zion, "Restorative Justice Practices of Native American, First Nation and Other Indigenous People of North America: Part One," interview by Laura Mirsky, International Institute of Restorative Practices, April 27, 2004, https://www.iirp.edu/news/restorative-justice-practices-of-native-american-first-nation-and-other-indigenous-people-of-north-america-part-one.

6   Howard Zehr, *The Little Book of Restorative Justice* (New York: Good Books, 2002).

7   Kaba and Hassan, *Fumbling Towards Repair*, 7. The authors credit this definition of harm reduction to "Queer and Transgender people of color, drug users, people in the sex trade and survivors of the HIV/AIDS epidemic."

Chapter 10

1   bell hooks, Barbara Love, adrienne maree brown, and Peter Block, among others, offer fresh and needed insights into the constituent elements of birthing transformative communities.

2   Mohan Jyoti Dutta, "A Culture-Centered Approach to Listening: Voices of Social Change," *International Journal of Listening* 28, no. 2 (2014): 67–81, https://doi.org/10.1080/10904018.2014.876266.

3   Grdina, Johnson, and Pereira, "Connecting Individual and Societal Change."

4   Frederic Laloux, *Reinventing Organizations: A Guide to Creating Organizations Inspired by the Next*

Stage of Human Consciousness (Brussels, Belgium: Nelson Parker, 2014).

5   David Sloan Wilson, *Does Altruism Exist? Culture, Genes, and the Welfare of Others* (New Haven, CT: Yale University Press).

6   In the United States, plans are under development to incorporate the latest science and trends in trauma-informed care into statewide action plans, and in Pennsylvania, this includes an effort to apply trauma-informed practices to the criminal justice system. Listening justly is a necessity for any of this hopeful and potentially transformative work to have effect.

7   Barbara Marx Hubbard, *Conscious Evolution: Awakening the Power of Our Social Potential* (Novato, CA: New World Library, 1998), 10.

8   James O'Dea, *The Conscious Activist: Where Activism Meets Mysticism* (London: Watkins Publishing, 2014), 218.

9   Trim tabs are small, hinged, metal pieces attached to rudders, airplane wings, and elsewhere to turn or stabilize a ship or airplane with a small amount of pressure and movement. Tiny shifts yield major consequences.

10 See the work of Jean Houston.

Published titles include:

The Little Books of Justice & Peacebuilding present, in highly accessible
form, key concepts and practices from the fields of restorative justice, conflict
transformation, and peacebuilding. Written by leaders in these fields, they are
designed for practitioners, students, and anyone interested in justice, peace, and
conflict resolution.

The Little Books of Justice & Peacebuilding series is a cooperative effort
between the Center for Justice and Peacebuilding of Eastern Mennonite
University and publisher Good Books.